**PRENTICE-HALL SERIES
IN COUNSELING AND HUMAN DEVELOPMENT**
Norman R. Stewart, *Consulting Editor*

ADAPTIVE COUNSELING IN SCHOOLS
Rothney

CHANGING CHILDREN'S BEHAVIOR
Krumboltz and Krumboltz

COUNSELING STRATEGIES AND OBJECTIVES
Hackney and Nye

CRITICAL INCIDENTS IN SCHOOL COUNSELING
Calia and Corsini

THE HELPING RELATIONSHIP: PROCESS AND SKILLS
Brammer

MAKING VOCATIONAL CHOICES
Holland

Counseling Strategies and Objectives

HAROLD HACKNEY
Purdue University

SHERILYN NYE
University of Tennessee

PRENTICE-HALL, INC., Englewood Cliffs, New Jersey

Library of Congress Cataloging in Publication Data

HACKNEY, HAROLD
    Counseling strategies and objectives.

    (Prentice-Hall series in counseling and development)
    1. Counseling.   I. Nye, Sherilyn, joint
author.   II. Title.
BF637.C6H25   361.3′2   72-12841
ISBN 0-13-183285-9
ISBN 0-13-183277-8 (pbk)

Printed in the United States of America

10   9   8   7   6   5   4   3   2   1

Prentice-Hall International, Inc., London
Prentice-Hall of Australia, Pty., Ltd., Sydney
Prentice-Hall of Canada, Ltd., Toronto
Prentice-Hall of India Private Limited, New Delhi
Prentice-Hall of Japan, Inc., Toyko

Contents

7

8

9

10

11

12

Preface

Counseling Strategies and Objectives originally was written for use by the counselor-trainee about to begin his first contacts with clients through practicum or some similar experience. The need for such a book became increasingly evident as we assessed the needs of our students. Many of them could describe quite well what they should do in the interview. However, when faced with another human being who was seeking professional assistance, their knowledge suddenly seemed vague, abstract, and for all practical purposes, almost useless.

Indeed, we became weary of the exclamation: "I've read all those counseling theories but now what do I actually say and do in the interview process?" Increasingly we realized the need for a book that delineates and gives practice in some specific counseling strategies that pertain directly to the interview process.

One additional realization, beyond the need for practicality, was the need for a book that would bring together the most important aspects of various counseling theories. Again, we were struck by the anxiety state generated in beginning counselors who, after exposure to many seemingly

divergent counseling approaches, could find no way to integrate common-
alities of the process into a meangful whole. Therefore we have attempted
to formulate a counseling model that draws upon similarities among theories,
emphasizing basic elements common to all theoretical approaches. We call
this a discrimination model.

Then, as the generation of the book continued, and its use increased,
we realized that the value of such a book is not limited solely to the counselor-trainee. The emphasis on the relationship, communication, and discrimination processes makes this book a valuable tool for anyone engaged
in a helping profession, regardless of its nature or level. Thus, the book is
not only intended for counselors-in-training, but also for those individuals
in para-professional and in-service training in other areas related to counseling. Toward this end, we anticipate finding the book in use by residence hall
counselors, mental health workers, and social workers as well.

In conclusion, we would like to point out that we began in much the
same place as beginning counselors, unsure of ourselves, feeling a bit pre-
sumptuous at the notion that we could help others, sometimes questioning
our motives. We doubt that these feelings ever disappear, though they do
decrease greatly in intensity. One feeling that does not decrease is the
desire to enhance the value of our contacts with others.

ACKNOWLEDGEMENTS

Much of the information in this book has grown out of the recent research in counseling and human behavior. It is difficult to say which studies
came first in our thinking. Certainly the research on behavioral change
through operant conditioning was an early influence. We are indebted to
people such as Frederick Kanfer, Leonard Krasner, Edward Pepyne, John
Krumboltz, Carl Thoresen, Ray Hosford, and Thomas Crowley. Their work
has presented a structural basis for examining communication and change.
This line of research led us to conclude that counseling and therapy are
more than the establishment of therapeutic conditions. Thus, we begin this
book with several assumptions about the counseling process:

1. That the counselor is an intervening agent in the client's world of concerns and trouble.
2. That the counselor's behavior, verbal and otherwise, is the vehicle for
   intervention, and
3. That the nature of this intervention may be viewed as either desirable
   or undesirable by the client, depending upon its relationship to the
   client's goals.

A second research thrust that has been highly influential has been the factor analytic studies which led to the development of counselor verbal-response classes or topics. The most dominant figure in this area has been Jules Zimmer, a researcher, teacher, and friend of the highest order.

We must also acknowledge the influence of Allen Ivey. His emphasis upon the training process through micro-counseling provided us with further direction in our attempt to apply research findings to the practice of counselor training. As we have assessed the impact these significant people have had upon our thinking, it has become apparent to us that we have stood upon their shoulders to gain our own perspective.

Still another group of people has influenced us by their presence, support and their friendship. These are our colleagues and friends. To Allen Segrist, Bruce Shertzer, Dick Nelson, Shelley Stone, Allan Dye, and our colleagues at the University of Tennessee, we say thank you very much. We want to express a special word of appreciation to Mrs. Virginia Wells, who turned our hieroglyphics into a manuscript.

Finally, we wish to express our sincere appreciation and gratitude to Norman Stewart, our Consulting Editor, whose suggestions and encouragement greatly facilitated our own thinking.

HAROLD HACKNEY
SHERILYN NYE

Lafayette, Indiana

*Counseling Strategies
and Objectives*

1

Introduction

This is a book about counseling strategies. It is also about helping people. The current emphasis in counseling on accountability clearly indicates the need to examine our efforts in terms of goals and outcomes. On the other hand, we would certainly be remiss if we failed to keep foremost in our thinking the human element that makes counseling a unique experience. Therefore, although each chapter tends to focus upon specific objectives and behaviors characteristic of the counseling process, these techniques and goals are subservient to the human relationship that develops in successful counseling.

Counseling is both unique and predictable. It is unique in the sense that one rarely can anticipate the kinds of problems and concerns that a particular client will present. Experienced counselors and therapists often admit that they are frequently surprised by the topics their clients introduce. At the same time, counseling is predictable in the sense that many problems or concerns are widely shared by people. Everyone has been depressed, felt defeated, indecisive, confused. Expressing these feelings often is difficult, and there are specific things the counselor can do to make it easier for the client to express such feelings. Thus we can predict that if the counselor is able to recognize and respond to the subtle cues of the client, he will soon have the client talking about his feelings. We know that this prediction is true. If it were not true, the accumulated experience of the counselor would be of little value.

Therefore, the book will focus upon those strategies and behaviors which grow out of the accumulated experiences of counselors. At the same time, an effort will be made to place these counselor activities in a humanistic perspective. Toward this end, the book begins and ends with a consideration of human qualities. Chapter Two attempts to identify those human and very normal behaviors which, under most conditions, would be inappropriate in the counseling interview. Chapter Ten concludes with those human qualities that facilitate and enhance the building of positive growth relationships. Chapter Eleven identifies the specific challenges which face you, the counselor, as you integrate the material contained in this book.

Sandwiched between are chapters that deal with problems over which most beginning counselors lose sleep. How does one counsel the silent client? What is the counselor's impact upon the client, and conversely, what is the client's impact upon the counselor? How does one get the interview started? How does the counselor get the client to talk about his feelings? How do the counselor and client establish goals? How does one terminate the interview? the counseling relationship?

Each chapter has been written using a structure that has come to be known as "programmed." It is intended to give the reader an opportunity to assess his progress as he incorporates a body of knowledge into his own thinking. Questions are related to the immediately preceding material. Answers to questions will be found on the same page as the question or on the following page. The main purpose of the questions is to focus your attention on the material with the ultimate goal of retaining what you have read. If this approach disturbs you, feel free to "cheat". It is all right to look ahead to the answers. On the other hand, you might find that this programmed approach permits you to acquire new information in a rather painless and even pleasant way. Don't knock it until you've tried it!

If you are using this book as a member of a class or in-service group, you may find that some members of the group proceed more quickly than others. This is a natural phenomenon and should not be interpreted to mean that the faster learner will make a better counselor. Therefore, do not be concerned if you should find yourself proceeding at a slower pace than some of your colleagues. The value of a programmed text is that you may proceed *at your own pace*.

Most of the chapters conclude with a set of exercises. These are structured experiences that permit a first-hand encounter with the strategies. The exercises can be carried out in any way you choose, although we would suggest that one good way is to organize into groups of three. One member assumes the role of counselor (or listener), a second member assumes the role of client (or talker), and the third member acts as observer. The client role should be a real one. This exercise is of greater value when the talker shares real concerns with the listener. The observer role is important because, although he does not actively participate, at the conclusion of the exercise he provides feedback that can be most useful in helping the other two gain insights into their interaction. The roles should be rotated until each member of the triad has an opportunity to experience each role. At the conclusion, it would be meaningful to discuss the experience in the light of what you believe you have learned about yourself and about each role. You may find it useful to video- or audio-tape as many of these kinds of interactions as possible for an excellent feedback source.

Finally, the behaviors and strategies should be related to "real-life" situations. You will find that many of the strategies will cast you in the role of "good listener." Such a role can be appreciated by your friends and associates. At the same time it can give you an opportunity to incorporate your newly acquired knowledge into your existing life style.

2

Reduction of Inappropriate Social Behavior

Counseling, though incorporating some characteristics common to all processes of human interaction, nevertheless retains certain unique characteristics of its own. Consequently, particular kinds of social behavior displayed in many daily events are not appropriate for the counseling setting, in that they are behaviors which do not facilitate the attainment of counseling goals and client change. The aim of this chapter is to assist you in the assessment of your impact on others, to identify interfering social patterns in the counseling setting, and to learn more facilitative communication patterns.

Patterson[1] has pointed out certain behaviors that are *not* synonymous with the process of effective counseling. Among these are the following:

1. Counseling is not the giving of information, though information may be present.

[1] C. H. Patterson, *The Counselor in the School: Selected Readings* (New York: McGraw-Hill, 1967), p. 219.

2. Counseling is not the giving of advice.
3. Counseling is not the influencing of attitudes, beliefs, and behaviors by persuading, admonishing, threatening, or compelling without the use of physical force.
4. Counseling is not the selection and assignment of individuals to jobs.
5. Counseling is not interviewing, though interviewing is involved.

What, then, is counseling? Counseling is the helping relationship, which includes (1) someone seeking help, (2) someone willing to give help, who is (3) capable of, or trained to, help (4) in a setting which permits that help to be given and received. Although there are many counseling approaches that would fit this set of criteria, certain common elements exist within all these approaches:

1. Counseling involves responding to both the feelings and thoughts of the client. Or, thinking of this in another way, the counselor deals with both attitudes and behaviors of the client. Existing theoretical approaches differ with respect to emphasis and order of responsiveness to feelings and behavior. Some approaches (client centered; existential) favor an emphasis on feelings; others (rational-emotive; reality therapy; behavioral) emphasize the importance of behaviors and actions. An eclectic counseling model, however, would acknowledge the importance of being able to identify and respond appropriately to both feeling states and behaviors.
2. Counseling involves a basic acceptance of the client's perceptions and feelings, irrespective of outside evaluative standards. In other words, the counselor must first accept where the client is at the present time before dealing with where the client could be. Considering this from the client's point of view, he needs the counselor's understanding of his current situation and concerns before he can anticipate growth and change in a new direction.

---

1. According to Patterson, counseling is something other than the

giving of _____ or _____.

---

3. Confidentiality and privacy constitute essential ingredients in the counseling setting. Physical facilities that preserve this quality are important. Therefore counseling is not typically conducted in the counselor's home, the local coffee shop, or other informal, non-confidential settings.
4. Counseling is voluntary; it is not usually effective when it is something that the client is required to do. Regardless of how the client is referred,

the counselor never uses coercion as a means of obtaining or continuing with a client.

5. London [2] notes that the counselor operates with a conservative bias against communicating to the client detailed information about his own life. Although there are times when counselor self-disclosure is appropriate, generally the counselor does not complicate the interview by focusing attention on his personal life and concerns.

6. One skill underlying all systems of counseling is that of communication. Counselors and clients alike continually transmit and receive verbal and nonverbal messages during the interview process. Therefore awareness of and sensitivity to the kinds of messages present is an important prerequisite for counselor effectiveness.

The correct answers to Item 1 are: **information** or **advice**. Re-read page 4 if you missed this item or are confused about it.

---

2. Certain common elements exist within all counseling approaches. These include lack of evaluation, focus on the client, confidentiality, and an emphasis on _____ content.

Basic to all counseling approaches is ongoing communication between the counselor and client. Communication is conducted by verbal, nonverbal, and paralanguage modalities. That is, communication exists with words, with facial expressions, gestures, body movements, and with tone of voice, rate of speech, pitch and so forth.

The correct answer to Item 2 is **feeling** or **feelings** or **affective**. Refer to page 5 for a review of this topic.

---

3. Verbal, nonverbal and paralanguage _____ is a process basic to all counseling approaches.

---

[2] P. London, *The Modes and Morals of Psychotherapy* (New York: Holt, Rinehart and Winston), 1964, p. 45.

COMMUNICATION PATTERNS

There are basically three kinds of communication patterns which are common in ordinary social intercourse but inappropriate in the counseling relationship. These may be identified as follows:

1. under-participation
2. over-participation
3. distracting participation

The counselor who is an under-participator may have a fear of involvement either with the client or with a certain problem area. The under-participatory counselor's verbal communication is not direct; there is often too much reliance on the nonverbal. The under-participatory counselor may convey to the client that he is not able or willing to help him, thus reducing the client's faith in the counselor and in the counseling process. Behaviorally, an under-participatory counselor can be described as follows:

Nonverbal characteristics:

1. May appear stiff; little body movement.
2. Body position often pulled away from the client.
3. Eyes are often averted and downcast.
4. Sometimes evidence of stooped shoulders, shrugging of shoulders.

Verbal characteristics:

1. Verbal speech characterized by monosyllabic responses or phrases rather than complete sentences.
2. Verbal speech often is not continuous.
3. Sometimes evidence of self-deprecating statements.
4. Verbal responses are primarily reflective in nature.

Paralanguage characteristics:

1. Tone of voice is soft and weak; responses sometimes trail off into silence.

The correct answer to Item 3 is **communication** or **communicating**. See page 6 for review.

4. The under-participatory counselor discourages the client from

_____ **him which reduces the counselor's potential to help.**

The counselor who is an over-participator may use this response style as a way to cover up feelings of anxiety in the interview. To exert control is often used as an anxiety reduction tool. This counselor relies heavily on action-oriented, confrontative statements and jumps to conclusions without much awareness of the client's feelings. Behaviorally, an over-participatory counselor can be characterized as follows:

Nonverbal characteristics:

1. Often a great deal of body movement; many gestures, fidgeting.
2. Much animation and expression, often to the point of being distracting.

Verbal characteristics:

1. Verbal speech characterized by a high output of words, often a compulsive flow of verbiage.
2. Verbal speech often laden with detail and repetition.
3. Length of response frequently exceeds length of preceding client response.

Paralanguage characteristics:

1. Rate of verbal speech is quite fast; pauses between sentences are few.
2. Tone of voice often high and loud.

The correct answer to Item 4 is **trusting** or **believing**. If the answer is not obvious, re-read page 7.

5. The over-participatory counselor, though he may appear to be

in control of the interview, is probably more _____ **than one might first think.**

There is another kind of communication pattern inappropriate for the counseling setting exhibited by some counselors. This is the counselor who exhibits a distracting kind of participation in the interview. He may be involved, but he has difficulty focusing on the client and responding to the primary stimuli emitted by the client. The counselor who is a distracting participator frequently responds to secondary and irrelevant aspects of the client's communication. Behaviorally this kind of inappropriate participation can be described as follows:

Nonverbal characteristics:

1. Inappropriate smiling, frequent nervous laughter.

Verbal characteristics:

1. Speech characterized by distractors; speaker does not respond to the stimulus at hand but to a secondary stimulus.
2. Speech further characterized by shifts in topics.
3. Speech often centers on others rather than the client, and the past rather than the immediate present.

The correct answer to Item 5 is **anxious** or **nervous**. See page 8 again for review.

---

6. Some counselors may be involved in the interview, but their participation is _____ **in that it centers on others than the client, and on secondary and irrelevant aspects of the client's communication.**

Below are some client statements followed by counselor responses. Describe each counselor response by (a) whether or not he responds to the client's statements, and if not (b) the nature of his inappropriate response, such as shift of topics, focus on others, or focus on past.

A. CLIENT: "I think I just have to go away for awhile. The pressure is really building up."

COUNS.:   "What would Bob say to that?"

B. CLIENT: "She doesn't really care anymore, and I've got to learn to accept that."

Couns.: "You are fairly sure that she doesn't care."

C. Client: "Money is the biggest problem I have in school. The grades aren't that hard to get."

Couns.: "What did you do last year?"

D. Client: "The job I have isn't fun, but I'm afraid if I quit, I might not get another job."

Couns.: "Jobs are really getting hard to find."

The correct answer to Item 6 is **distracting**. Go back to page 9 if this was unclear.

Here are the answers to the exercises at the bottom of page 9:

A. This response probably was inappropriate. The counselor seems to have topic-jumped by bringing up Bob. In addition, the counselor ignored the client's referral to the pressure and its effect upon him.

B. This response is appropriate, though it isn't the only possible appropriate response. The counselor is responding directly to what the client said.

C. This is an inappropriate response. The counselor didn't respond to any of the key words in the client's statement (money, problem, grades). Instead the counselor decided to do some history-taking.

D. This is an inappropriate response. The client is talking about his feelings ("isn't fun"; "afraid"). The counselor's response has nothing to do with the client. It is more like a social commentary on the current economic scene.

Now that you are aware of behavioral descriptions of inappropriate social behaviors and communication patterns in the counseling setting, can you deduce some appropriate behaviors? Be specific as to both nonverbal (face, eyes, tone of voice, rate of speech, etc.) body language (head, arms, body position, etc.) and verbal components (choice of words, types of responses, etc.). List them on a separate sheet of paper.

Discuss what you specified as appropriate counselor behaviors and communication patterns. Try some out. You may find that you will need to un-learn some behaviors and re-learn some others. This will take a little time and practice until you feel completely comfortable with your new styles. With a partner, decide which of the following appropriate counselor behaviors are not present in your current repertoire. Set behavioral goals for yourself. What is it that you would like to be able to do as a result of your newly acquired learnings? Share this with your partner. Make some commitment about the kinds of things you are going to do this week to implement your goals. Your partner should do the same thing. This way you and your partner can give each other feedback about goal attainment as you continue to interact throughout the remainder of the exercises. Perhaps some of the appropriate counselor behaviors you listed for the exercise included:

facial animation
good eye contact
occasional head nodding
soft, firm tone of voice
occasional smiling
occasional gesturing with hands
moderate rate of speech
response to primary stimulus of client communication
verbal speech centers on client and on immediate present
occasional use of minimal verbal reinforcers, e.g. "mm-hmm."

RECOMMENDED READINGS

GINOTT, HAIM G., *Between Parent and Child.* New York: Avon Books, 1969.

Although this book is written to and for parents, it is essential reading for the future child counselor. It focuses upon communication between adult and child, suggesting ways that you can learn to talk "childrenese".

GORDON, THOMAS, *Parent Effectiveness Training.* New York: Peter Wyden and Company, 1971.

This book highlights techniques of communication skills, particularly those kinds of statements designed to communicate understanding of feelings.

LOEFFLER, DOROTHY, "Counseling and the Psychology of Communication," *Personnel and Guidance Journal,* 48 (April, 1970), 629–36.

Loeffler discusses the ways in which people communicate, the importance of communication in counseling, and describes six inappropriate or ineffective counselor communication patterns. This is a "must" article for you to read and discuss.

STRONG, STANLEY; TAYLOR, RONALD; BRATTON, JOSEPH; and LOPER, RODNEY, "Non-verbal Behavior and Perceived Counselor Characteristics," *Journal of Counseling Psychology,* 18 (November, 1971), 554–61.

The authors studied counselors' nonverbal behavior and found that certain gestural, postural, and other nonverbal movements had a negative effect on how they were perceived. The study suggests that there are inappropriate nonverbal behaviors that the counselor must also be aware of.

3

Counselor Reinforcing Behavior

Have you ever tried to talk to someone who was fiddling with a pencil, staring around the room, or seeming to be interested in something other than what you were saying? If so, you can recall how this made you feel. You may have interpreted the other person's behavior as lack of interest in what you were saying. And, that seeming to be the case, you probably were not inclined to continue the conversation. It could be said then, that your talking did not get reinforced by the other person. The lack of reinforcement probably led to your ceasing to talk, or to the extinction of your verbal behavior. This can be described in other ways as well. It could be said that the listener lacked any involvement or commitment, or that the interaction could not develop into a helping relationship under such conditions.

This chapter deals with the skills of counselor reinforcing behavior. It involves an awareness of the client's communications and, in turn, a communication of your attentiveness to the client. Attentiveness is related to other counselor attitudes, such as involvement and empathy. Price and Iverson found in their research that a high commitment on the part of the counselor to the helping relationship seems to be much more facilitative than low commitment.[1] Attentiveness is one way of communicating this commitment and involvement to the client. Other studies indicate that counselor interest and commitment appear to be related to clients' and observers' perception of the counselor's empathy [2] and that attentiveness, empathy, and affectional nurturance are all related to one another.[3] Furthermore, low-level reinforcers such as interest and approval are more generalized than overt reactions such as "That's good."

---

1. When you are attentive to the other person, it can be said that

your attentiveness is _____ the other person to continue talking.

ATTENTIVENESS

Attentiveness is communicated primarily through three channels: facial expressions, bodily positions and movement, and verbal response.[4] These communication modes offer cues to the client as to the level of acceptance, approval, agreement, rejection, or indifference associated with reinforcing behavior.[5] Do you prefer having someone look at you when you talk to them? When you are telling someone what you think, if they frown, what is your probable reaction? If you feel strongly about something and the other person doesn't seem to care about it, are you likely to continue telling the person about your feelings?

The correct answer to Item 1 is **reinforcing** or **rewarding**. If you do not understand how this can be the correct answer, it would help to re-read page 13. If you have the correct answer, please continue.

---

[1] L. A. Price and M. A. Iverson, "Students' Perception of Counselors with Varying Statuses and Role Behaviors in the Initial Interview," *Journal of Counseling Psychology,* 16 (1969), 469–75.

[2] P. F. Caracena and J. R. Vicory, "Correlates of Phenomenological and Judged Empathy," *Journal of Counseling Psychology,* 16 (1969), 510–15.

[3] H. L. Hackney, A. E. Ivey, and E. R. Oetting, "Attending, Island, and Hiatus Behavior: A Process Conception of Counselor and Client Interaction," *Journal of Counseling Psychology,* 17 (1970), 342–46.

[4] Allen Ivey, *Microcounseling: Innovations in Interviewing Training* (Springfield, Illinois: C. C. Thomas, 1971), 41.

[5] Hackney, *et al.,* "Attending, Island, and Hiatus Behavior," pp. 342–46.

2. Reinforcing behaviors are an important way to communicate the counselor's _____ or commitment to the client.

The counselor's behavior can contribute to the client's feeling of security. This increased sense of security, which occurs at the same time the client is talking about himself, can become a self-reinforcing phenomenon. Have you ever entered a new activity and found yourself to be very nervous and unsure at the outset? As you continued the activity, and nothing bad (perhaps even some good things) happened, did you gain in self-confidence? Did you put more of yourself into the activity as a result? Did it grow easier to become involved?

The correct answer to Item 2 is **involvement**. If this correct answer is not familiar to you, it would help to review page 14 again.

3. As you are learning the skills of reinforcing behavior, keep in mind the three communication channels that permit you to respond to the client. These three channels are _____ expressions, _____ position, and _____ responses.

THE EFFECT OF FACIAL EXPRESSIONS

The counselor uses facial expressions to reinforce client behavior in three primary ways: eye contact, head nods, and manipulation of facial muscles to produce frowns, smiles, quizzical looks, indifference, etc.

The correct answers to Item 3 are **facial** expressions, **bodily** position, and **verbal** responses. If these answers are not the same as your answers, refer to the paragraph on page 14.

4. If the counselor's behavior, facially, bodily, and verbally, communicates to the client a sense of acceptance, commitment, and involvement, this can help increase the client's sense of _____ _____.

Eye Contact

What is good eye contact? You need not gaze fixedly at a client, but at the same time, frequent breaks in eye contact communicate non-attentiveness. A varied use of eye contact is more effective. Look at the client when he is talking. Occasionally permit your eyes to drift to an object away, *but not far away,* from the client. Then return your eyes to the client. Let yourself be natural. Do not be afraid to invite the client into the world of your vision.

Perhaps you can better grasp the effects of eye contact by participating in the following dyadic exercise. One of you should be the talker and the other the listener. While the talker speaks, the listener should listen, but avoid eye contact with the speaker. What are the effects on the speaker? This time try it again, but maintain eye contact with the speaker as described in the previous section. What effects does this have? Now reverse roles and again discuss the results.

The correct answer to Item 4 is **security**, or **safety**. The client's feeling of security is discussed on page 15.

5. Frequent breaks in eye contact are negatively reinforcing since they communicate _____.

The Head Nod

Affirmative head nods can indicate to the client that you are listening and being attentive. When overdone however, they can become distracting. You do want the client to be aware of your attentiveness. The use of occasional head nods, paired with good eye contact, will reassure (reinforce) the client of your involvement and commitment.

The correct answer to Item 5 is **non-attentiveness** or **non-involvement**. This response was discussed on page 16.

---

6. Occasional affirmative head nods suggest to the client that you

are _____.

Animation

Animation in facial expressions gives the client the feeling that you are alert and responding to his communications. It may be that your facial expressions serve as a kind of mirror for the client's feelings. Generally your facial expression should reflect the kind and intensity of the feeling being expressed by the client. Certainly an absence of facial expression (the proverbial dead-pan) will suggest a lack of interest, awareness, or mental presence to the client. Again, it is possible to be overly expressive. A smile is almost always more appropriate than a laugh (particularly when it is a nervous laugh). A continual smile becomes a negative stimulus. Frequent frowns can communicate disapproval. Occasional frowns, on the other hand, communicate the counselor's failure to follow or understand a particular point, and are therefore useful.

With a partner, designate one of you as the speaker and the other as the listener. While the speaker shares one of his concerns with you, your tasks as the listener are as follows:

1. Do not respond with any facial expression or animation whatsoever while the speaker is talking; maintain complete impassivity.
2. Respond with a facial reaction which is opposite of the feelings and concerns being emitted by the speaker. For example, if the speaker is talking seriously, smile and look happy. Discuss together the effects of this facial responsiveness.
3. Respond with facial animation and expressions that mirror the kind and intensity of feelings being expressed by the speaker. Discuss the different results produced by this style. Reverse the roles and again discuss the differential effects. What do you conclude about facial attentiveness as a result of this exercise?

The correct answer to Item 6 is **listening** or **being attentive**. If you missed this answer, you might refer back to page 16.

7. The overuse of facial expressions can produce a _____ effect.

The key to bodily communication is to relax, physically. You will find yourself more able to listen to the client if you feel relaxed rather than tense, and your client will feel less tense if you do not appear tense. In order to get your body relaxed, you must find a position that is comfortable under non-stress conditions. You cannot bend your body into a pretzel and relax the muscles at the same time. Secondly, you must concentrate upon something other than yourself (preferably what the client is saying).

The correct answer to Item 7 is **negative** or **undesired**.

8. When you are aware of your own body tension, it means that

you are unable to give your client your full _____.

If your position is relaxed, you will be more able to move around at times and make use of expressive gestures without moving and gesturing to the point of distraction. The following exercise may help you to achieve a desired state of relaxation.

EXERCISE 1: RELAXING.   While sitting down, raise your hands and arms three to four inches above the arm rests of the chair, and then let them drop. Feel the tension flow out of the arms. Let your back and buttocks contact as much of the chair as possible. Feel the chair pressing against your body. Tense the muscles in your legs and then release the tension. Repeat this tensing and releasing several times. Now take three or four deep breaths and after each breath slowly release the air from your lungs. Do you feel more relaxed than when you started? Try to exercise again, this time without any interruptions between different body exercises.

The correct answer to Item 8 is **attention.** If you missed this response, it would help for you to re-read page 18 and think about the implications of a tense appearance.

---

9. **Topic-jumping suggests to the client that you have your own ideas about what he should discuss. This tends to place the**

_____ **for topic choice on you.**

VERBAL BEHAVIOR

The things you say will have immediate impact upon the client. Many studies have shown that the counselor's responses can mold and shape the direction of the client's responses. There are several points to be considered in terms of your verbal impact. First, fit your comments or questions into the context of the topic at hand. Don't interrupt the client or jump topics. Stay with the topic the client introduces and help him develop and pursue it. This implies more than a technique; it is a highly conscious awareness of what is going on between you and your client. See if you can practice verbal following in the exercise below.

The correct answer to Item 9 is **responsibility.** Can you see how this would happen?

EXERCISE 2: VERBAL BEHAVIOR. In the roles of counselor/client, choose a partner and sit in pairs, back-to-back. Concentrate on using verbal reinforcing behaviors as you listen to the other person for five minutes. You cannot turn around; no eye contact, no gestures, only verbal responses. After five minutes, switch roles. You talk for five minutes and the other person will listen and respond verbally.

The purpose of this exercise is to learn to communicate your attentiveness, involvement, empathy, and commitment by solely verbal means. Now discuss with your partner the limitations and values you experienced in your verbal interaction.

Vocal Characteristics

The use of a well-modulated, unexcited vocal tone and pitch will reassure the client of your own comfort with his problems. The use of intermittent one-word phrases (minimal verbal stimuli) serves much the same purpose as the head-nod and eye contact. These are verbal signs that you are listening and following what the client is saying. The more common minimal verbal stimuli are: "Mm-hmm", "Mmm", "Yes", "I see", etc. There is one hazard which should be mentioned. Overuse of these verbal stimuli can produce a "parrot-like" effect that has negative results. Later chapters will show how you can use minimal verbal stimuli and the other types of reinforcing behaviors to assist the client in developing his thinking.

---

10. Minimal verbal stimuli tell the client that you are _____

_____ **to what he is saying.**

In summary, one of your goals in the counseling setting is to listen attentively and to communicate this attentiveness through the use of eye contact, intermittent head-nods, a variety of facial expressions, relaxed posture, modulated voice, minimal verbal stimuli, and verbal comments that follow the client's topics. The effect of this communication will be to reinforce the client's verbal behavior, comfort, and potential to examine and understand himself.

The correct answer to Item 10 is **listening.**

RECOMMENDED READINGS

DILLEY, JOSIAH; LEE, JAMES; and VERRILL, ELEANOR, "Is Empathy Ear-to-Ear or Face-to-Face?" *Personnel and Guidance Journal,* 50 (November, 1971), 188–91.

The authors describe a study comparing counselor empathy in the traditional setting to counselor empathy when the counseling was conducted over the telephone. The article raises some interesting issues about how empathy is communicated.

HACKNEY, H. L.; IVEY, A. E.; and OETTING, E. R., "Attending, Island, and Hiatus Behavior: A Process Conception of Counselor and Client Interaction," *Journal of Counseling Psychology,* 17 (July, 1970), 342–46.

The authors discuss how counselor attending behavior, verbal and nonverbal, affect and reinforce the kinds of topics the client discusses.

KORN, CLAIRE V., "Refusing Reinforcement," in J. D. Krumboltz and C. E. Thoreson (eds.), *Behavioral Counseling, Cases and Techniques.* New York: Holt, Rinehart and Winston, 1966, 45–48.

What is pleasing to one person may have the opposite effect on another. Using anecdotes from child counseling, Korn describes how verbal reinforcement sometimes fails.

KRASNER, LEONARD, "The Therapist as a Social Reinforcement Machine," in H. H. Strupp and L. Luborsky (eds.), *Research in Psychotherapy,* Vol. II. Baltimore: French-Bray Printing Co., 1962, 61–94.

Krasner describes many variables, including therapist behaviors, client variables, the setting, etc., and how these can be used to effect client change. The article is an excellent review of the research which has been done.

4

Using Silence

For most beginning counselors silence can be frightening. It seems to bring the total focus of attention upon them, revealing their most glaring weaknesses as counselors. At least this is how many beginning counselors relate their experience with silence. As a result, their tendency is to say something, anything, to prevent silence. Typically a question is asked. It is often a bad question, one which can be answered by a minimal response by the client. The answer to the question is relatively unimportant since the question was not well thought-out in the counselor's mind. The counselor may not even be listening to the answer. He may be preparing the next question!

Silence has a similar effect upon clients. They also perceive silence as a threatening condition and feel a need to respond, to fill the gaps of silence with talking. Because clients react to silence in this way, you can use silence as a counseling technique and as a way of responding to clients.

1. Counselors can use silence as a type of counseling _____

_____ .

One of the objectives of counseling, as described in Chapter Three, is to invite and encourage clients to talk. The purpose is to get to know the client's world, to begin collecting information about the client. Ideally this should be information that the client considers important. It is in this endeavor that silence can be used as a tool or a technique. By permitting silence to occur, you can communicate your desire to transfer to the client the responsibility for choosing topics. As you learn to tolerate silence without seeming to become anxious or distracted, the client will begin to realize that it is his responsibility to initiate topics.

Answer to Item 1 is **tool** or **technique.**

1. Silence becomes a technique when it is used to communicate the counselor's desire that the client assume _____ for topic selection.

Counselor silence can also be viewed as a type of response. Sometimes the client will ask questions in rapid succession. When this happens, it can be an attempt to transfer responsibility for the interview direction from himself to the counselor. It is as though he were saying "You make the decisions, you sit on the hot seat and talk for awhile." When this happens, silence is one of several ways in which you can meet the client's challenge. Often you will find that the client's questions are rhetorical. He may not even wait for your answer before asking another question. He is attempting to avoid the attention or spotlight which he feels silence produces.

Answer to Item 2 is **responsibility.**

3. Silence can be a type of counseling _____ .

USING SILENCE

There is no rule of thumb to help you know when to remain silent and when to interrupt a silence. Although some counselors may remain silent when the pause has been initiated by the client, sensitivity is required to judge what is best in a particular situation. Sometimes client-initiated silence means that the client is examining himself, seeking self-insight. It can mean that the client needs a moment to absorb some new insight. Or it can mean that the client is considering some new direction to take. All of these are good reasons for silence to occur.

On the other hand, client-initiated silence can mean that the client wishes to avoid the topic. Although the silence may not seem as productive to the client under this condition, there is still good reason to permit the silence to occur.

Answer to Item 3 is **response**.

---

4. Client-induced silence may mean that the client is using the silence to assimilate new _____.

Interpreting Client Silence

The reason behind a client-induced silence must be inferred. However, by watching the client, you will be able to gather some clues to what is happening. Is the client relaxed, are his eyes fixed upon something without being focused? This usually means he is thinking about something, examining a new idea, or ruminating around in his mind. Or is the client tense, appearing nervous, looking from one object to another and avoiding eye contact with you? This may mean that he is avoiding some topic or idea.

Answer to Item 4 is **insights, information** or **ideas**.

---

5. If the client is nervous and avoiding eye contact during a silence, it may mean that he is avoiding some _____.

Shertzer and Stone [1] note that greatly prolonged silence could be interpreted as sadistic if the counselor refuses to speak because he demands the initiation of all topics by the client. At first many clients will not be aware of their responsibility to initiate topics. The counselor will need to structure the relationship to a minimal level until the client learns the necessity of using his own initiative in the interview. This is one aspect of what is meant when it is said that you must teach the client to be a client. After this orientation, silence may be used as a way to place responsibility on the client.

Answer to Item 5 is **topic.**

6. If the counselor carries the use of silence to extremes, the client may interpret his behavior as _____.

Pacing the Interview

Silence can also be used to slow down the pace of the interview. It permits time for the client to gain understanding of his feelings. Even when the counselor is silent verbally, he can communicate his presence and understanding, nonverbally, to his client. Thus, you can give the client a sense of security and self-worth, even though you are not responding verbally to him.

Answer to Item 6 is **sadistic.**

EXERCISES

In our culture people often have to learn to be silent. Perhaps you find silence to be intense, uncomfortable. If so, team up with two other people. Let one person be the talker, you be the listener, and the third person can be the time-keeper. Invite the talker to talk about anything he wishes. You will listen and respond. The one restriction on your re-

[1] B. Shertzer and S. C. Stone, *Fundamentals of Counseling* (Boston: Houghton Mifflin, 1968), p. 374.

sponses is that you must wait 30 seconds between each response. The timer will signal when your 30 seconds have lapsed permitting you to respond again. As this becomes a tolerable limit of time to remain silent, gradually increase the "silent" time to 35 seconds, 40 seconds, etc. When you can listen for two to three minutes without discomfort, you can end the exercise.

5

Beginning
and Terminating
the Interview

The beginning counselor often experiences concerns about effectively opening and terminating an interview. Understanding of the processes involved at these interview points can assist you in feeling comfortable with both the beginning and the ending of an interview. In opening an interview, it is important to provide conditions that encourage the client to *talk*.

At the outset of an interview, the counselor must:

1. Reduce the client's initial anxiety to a level which permits him to begin talking about himself.
2. Refrain from excessive talking, which restricts the client's talking.
3. Listen carefully to what the client is saying and attempt to reconstruct an image of his world as he is describing it.
4. Be aware that the client's choice of topics gives insights into his ranking of priorities.

---

1. In order for the client to begin talking in the interview, the counselor must provide ways to reduce the client's initial level

of _____.

In opening an interview, be on time for the client. This communicates your respect for him. The beginning point can be as simple as a smile on your part, paired with an introduction and a motion for the client to be seated, as in the following example:

"Hello, I'm _____. Please be seated." Once the introduction has been made the counselor should allow a brief pause, giving the client a chance to talk if he is prepared to begin.

The correct answer to Item 1 is **anxiety**. If you don't understand this, re-read page 27.

---

2. Being on time, beginning with an introduction and a smile on your part, can help the client to feel more _____.

PROVIDING INITIAL STRUCTURE

If several seconds of silence elapse and there is no indication the client is going to begin talking, the counselor will probably want to initiate some brief form of communication. In the initial (very first) interview it is often helpful in this situation to provide a minimal structure to the counseling process. *Structuring* has been defined as the way the counselor defines the nature, limits, roles, and goals within the counseling relationship.[1] It includes comments about time limits, confidentiality, possibilities and expectations, as well as observation and/or taping procedures. Structure reduces the anxiety of the client by describing the counseling process for the client and giving him an opportunity to check out his expectations.

---

[1] B. E. Shertzer and S. C. Stone, *Fundamentals of Counseling* (Boston: Houghton Mifflin, 1968), pp. 359–61.

The counselor may also want to emphasize the aspect of confidentiality to the new client. How much structure to provide depends on the client; the counselor must be sensitive to the degree of ambiguity each client can tolerate. However, even with very anxious clients, it is important that the counselor is not overly verbal at the outset of the interview. Some responsibility for talking must be placed on the client.

The correct answer to Item 2 is **comfortable** or **relaxed.** Refer back to page 28 if necessary.

---

3. In the initial interview the client's anxiety can be reduced by dealing with the ambiguity of the counseling process through

_____.

For example, after introducing himself and showing the client where he might sit, the counselor can provide some initial structure by saying:

> "We have about an hour together. I like to tape-record interviews with my clients. It's easier and less interfering than taking notes. I hope that won't bother you. I'm not sure what brings you here, but whatever it is that is bothering you will be treated in strict confidentiality. You can talk about anything you wish."

Types of responses the counselor could use after introductions if the client does not begin talking, are these:

> "It must be hard for you to know where to begin—but please feel free to go ahead."
>
> "You are probably wondering how we can start talking to each other."

These are essentially _encouraging_ responses; they acknowledge the difficulty of beginning but give a verbal suggestion at the same time. This link may be all that many clients need to begin talking. Some may go ahead and identify their reason for coming, blurting it out, or perhaps speaking hesitantly. Others may begin with "small talk", generally using it as an anxiety reduction tool.

The correct answer to Item 3 is **structuring.** Re-read page 29 if necessary.

---

4. If a client does not begin talking at the outset of an interview,

**the counselor can verbally _____ the client
to start talking about whatever he wants.**

How the client begins talking in large measure determines the way the counselor initially responds. Those clients who begin with "small talk" may make a comment about the weather, an event, or a story about another person they know. This is rarely their real reason for seeking counseling. Such topics tend to be conversational in nature and could be maintained as the content for a long time *if* the counselor responds as though it were a social conversation. Since counseling is not, it is important that the counselor does not reinforce this kind of communication, by initiating or encouraging social conversation as a way to achieve rapport. Generally the counselor will want to listen to what the client says until this conversational topic is exhausted—thus indicating his interest but not probing for deeper significance or encouraging further content of this sort.

The answer to Item 4 is **encourage**. Refer back to page 29 for more information.

5. Some clients may voluntarily identify their reasons for seeking counseling; others may begin with small talk. While the counselor listens to the client's topic, it is not helpful to encourage any

**kind of _____ in the
interview.**

ENCOURAGING THE CLIENT
TO CHOOSE A TOPIC

After initial topics have been exhausted, the client will usually provide some indication of the direction he wants to take, based on his reasons for seeking counseling. This transition is often recognized by a *pause* in the interaction—which can serve as a signal that the client is ready to talk about his goals and concerns. The counselor should thus respect this pause. An extended pause can often be an anxious time for the client, and an occasional client may remain suspended between the initial conversation and his reason for seeking counseling. If the pause becomes extended (several minutes), the counselor can provide a further stimulus for client communication with the use of an *unstructured invitation*, such as: "You probably have some important things you want to talk about." This kind of statement encourages the client to talk about his reasons for seeking help but leaves the specific area open for the client to identify.

The correct answer to Item 5 is **social conversation.** If you don't understand why, refer to page 30.

---

6. **The transition from social conversation to the client's identifica-**

   tion of his concerns is often recognizable by a _____
   which should generally be respected by the counselor unless it becomes extended.

If the unstructured invitation confuses the client, it can be clarified even further as in the following example:

> "I thought you might have some other things you want to bring up besides what we've been talking about."

The important point is this: provide an opportunity for the client to talk but let the topic be determined by the client.

The correct answer to Item 6 is **pause.** If you need to pause to think about this, see page 30.

SUMMARIES OF COUNSELOR STRATEGIES
FOR OPENING AN INTERVIEW

The Unstructured Invitation

This is an appropriate counselor style to be used at the beginning of an interview. This strategy has two purposes:

1. It gives the client an opportunity to talk.
2. It prevents the counselor from identifying the topic the client needs to discuss.

An unstructured invitation is essentially a statement in which the counselor encourages the client to begin talking about whatever is of concern to him. Examples of unstructured invitations are the following:

"Please feel free to go ahead and begin."
"Where would you like to begin today?"
"Talk about whatever you want to."
"You probably have some things you want to discuss."
"Is there something particular you want to talk about?"

Silence

Pauses and periods of silence are common in the beginning of an interview when things are just getting underway. Silence on the client's part may indicate he is deciding how to begin and is thinking through what to say. It is important for the counselor to be comfortable with silences; otherwise, in his insecurity, he tends to overtalk or to bombard the client with questions, thus shifting the focus from the client to the counselor.

Restatement

Although it is important for the counselor to maintain a listening role, there are certain kinds of responses which communicate not only that the counselor is listening, but also that the counselor is a person with an active role. The restatement is one of these responses. It is essentially a repetition by the counselor of the main thought or feeling expressed by the client's communication. An example is the following interaction:

Client: "I don't know whether to stay in school or to drop out and get a job, but if I do, I don't know what kind of a job I can find."

Counselor: "You are wondering whether to stay in school or to drop out and work."

In this example the client has communicated two thoughts: whether to stay in school or drop out to work, and uncertainty as to the possibility of finding a job. Research indicates that when the counselor uses a restatement it is easy to respond to the last thought emitted by the client—probably because of the immediacy. However, this is a poor criterion. It is better to pick out the primary thought or feeling of the client's communication, regardless of its position in the sentence. Pepyne[2] has observed that overuse of the restatement produces a "parrot-like" effect, but it can be used as frequently as once per minute and its effectiveness is retained.

---

7. There are three kinds of styles appropriate for opening an interview: the restatement, silence, and the (a) _____ _____. In the latter, the counselor (b) _____ the client to talk about whatever he would like.

Opening Subsequent Interviews

Once the counselor has established a relationship or rapport with his client, subsequent interviews require that he reinstate the relationship that has developed. Reinstating the relationship usually amounts to acknowledging the client's absence since the last interview, and communicating to the client his pleasure or satisfaction in seeing him again. This is done with a few short statements, such as "Hello, _____ _____. It's good to see you. How have things been (or) How have you been (or) How has your week been?" The counselor should be prepared for a certain amount of small talk. Don't worry that the small talk might consume the interview. This is just the client's way of getting back into his role of help-seeker. The important point is that the counselor will not need to go to the same lengths in establishing rapport as was necessary when counseling first was initiated.

The correct answers to Item 7 are (a) **unstructured invitation** and (b) **encourages, helps, or assists.**
See page 31 for a review.

---

[2] E. W. Pepyne, "The Control of Interview Content Through Minimal Social Stimuli" (Doctoral dissertation, The University of Massachusetts, 1963), p. 30.

TERMINATION OF AN INTERVIEW

The beginning counselor is often unsure about *when* to terminate and may feel ready to conclude either before or after the client is ready. A general rule of thumb is to limit the interview to a certain amount of time, such as forty-five or fifty minutes. Rarely does a counseling interview need to exceed an hour in length as both client and counselor have a saturation point.

There is also a minimal amount of time required for counseling to take place. Interviews that continue for no more than ten or fifteen minutes make it very difficult for the counselor to know enough about the client's concern to react appropriately. Indeed, counselors sometimes require five to ten minutes just to re-orient themselves and to change their frame of reference from their preceding attention-involving activity to the present activity of counseling.

Acceptance of time limits is especially important when the client has a series of interviews. Research has shown that clients, like everyone else, tend to postpone talking about their concerns as long as possible. Without time limits, the presumed one-hour interview may extend well beyond an hour as a result of this postponing tendency. It is the one area where the client can easily manipulate the counselor.

---

8. Termination of an interview is easier for both the counselor and

the client when _____ limits are observed.

Benjamin [3] has identified two factors basic to the closing process of the interview.

1. Both the client and the counselor should be aware that closing is taking place.
2. Termination concerns that which already has taken place; therefore no new material should be introduced or discussed at this phase of the interview. This can often be a touchy situation for the counselor when the client suddenly introduces a new topic at the end of the interview. Generally it is best to suggest discussing the new material at the next interview when more time is available as in the following example:
   "That sounds like a good place to begin next week."
   The rare exception to this would be when the client presents an urgent, immediate problem that he is really unable to handle.

[3] A. Benjamin, *The Helping Interview* (Boston: Houghton Mifflin, 1969), p. 30.

The correct answer to Item 8 is **time**. Re-read page 34 if necessary.

---

9. The counselor should avoid introducing or discussing any _____

_____ material at the termination phase of the interview.

Other Termination Strategies

Often a brief and to the point statement by the counselor will suffice for closing the interview; this statement usually will be a recognition that it is time to stop. This may be preceded by a pause or by a concluding kind of remark made by the client. Such counselor statements of this brief and explicit type are:

"It looks as if our time is up for today."
"Well, I think it's time to stop for today."

Another effective way is the use of *summarization*. Summarization provides continuity to the interview, is an active kind of counselor response, and often helps the client to hear what he has been saying. It is essentially a series of statements in which the counselor ties together the main points of the interview. It should be brief, to the point, and without interpretation. An example of a counselor using summarization at the end of an interview is the following:

"Essentially you have indicated that your main concern is with your family—and we have discussed how you might handle your strivings for independence without their interpreting this as rejection."

The correct answer to Item 9 is **new, additional,** or **different.** If this seems hazy to you, look over page 34 again.

---

10. There are several counselor strategies for terminating an interview effectively and efficiently. These include a brief statement, use of _____ by either counselor or client, and mutual feedback.

Another possible termination strategy is to ask the *client* to summarize; to state how he has understood what has been going on in the interview, as in the following example:

"As we're ending the session today, I'm wondering what you're taking with you—if you could summarize this, I think it would be helpful to both of us."

Mutual feedback involving both the client and counselor is another possible tool for termination of an interview. If plans and decisions have been made, it is often useful for both the counselor and client to clarify and verify the progress of the interview as in the following example:

Counselor: "I guess that's it for today and I'll also be thinking about the decision you're facing. As you understand it, what things do you want to do before our next session?"

The correct answer to Item 10 is **summarization**. If you got it, good! Otherwise, see page 35. Now check over your total understanding of strategies for opening and terminating an interview; try some out.

EXERCISES

Use the following triadic exercise to review styles of opening and terminating the interview. With one of you as the speaker, another as the respondent, and the third as observer, complete the following tasks: [4]

1. Speaker: Talk about yourself; share a concern with the listener.

   Listener: Respond to the speaker as if you were opening an interview. Try out the responses mentioned in the chapter: unstructured invitation, silence, minimal verbal activity, restatement.

   Observer: Observe the kinds of responses made by the listener. Keep a frequency count of the types of responses made. Share your report with the listener.

   Recycling: If as the listener you did not emit at least two of the four response classes in your interaction with the speaker, complete the interaction again.

   Role reversal: Reverse the roles and follow the same process.

2. Speaker: Continue to explore the same topic you introduced in

[4] Use the Observer Rating Chart on pages 38 and 39.

the above interaction.

Listener: Respond to the speaker as if you were terminating an interview. Try out at least one of the procedures mentioned in the section as approaches for termination of the interview: acknowledgment of time limits, summarization, or mutual feedback.

Observer: Observe the procedure for termination used by the listener. Share your report with the listener.

Recycling: If as the listener you did not emit any of the termination procedures, or if, for some reason, termination did not occur with your speaker, complete the interaction again.

Role reversal: Reverse the roles and follow the same process.

RECOMMENDED READINGS

BENJAMIN, ALFRED, *The Helping Interview.* Boston: Houghton Mifflin, 1969, Chapter Two, "Stages."

Benjamin makes some important statements to the beginning counselor about beginning and terminating the interview, and relates his remarks to the counselor's role. You will find Chapter Two to be very helpful.

DELANEY, DANIEL and EISENBERG, SHELDON, *The Counseling Process.* Chicago: Rand McNally, 1972, Chapter Two, "The Initial Session," and Chapter Seven, "Termination and Follow-up."

Using counselor behavior as a point of departure, the authors have provided an excellent description of the characteristics and conditions that influence the opening and the termination of the interview.

OBSERVER RATING CHART

OPENING THE INTERVIEW

Counselor Response	Type of Counselor Response			
	Unstructured Invitation	Silence	Minimal Verbal	Restatement
1.				
2.				
3.				
4.				
5.				
6.				

TERMINATING THE INTERVIEW

Counselor Response	Type of Counselor Response		
	Time Limits	Summarization	Mutual Feedback
1.			
2.			
3.			
4.			
5.			
6.			

6

Establishing Goals in Counseling

During the early stages of counseling the counselor needs to listen and understand the *conditions* that brought the client to him. As the counselor is able to understand the client's concerns, he should help the client to examine how these problems are related to the client's attitudes and behavior. Beyond this, the counselor and client should begin formulating tentative goals *together* that are directly related to the problems. As counseling continues, the original goals will be modified through better understanding of the problem, and the development of new attitudes and behaviors that will eliminate the particular problem.

What is a good counseling goal? Is it one that reflects a particular counseling theory? Should a counseling goal or objective suggest what the client will be like when the goal is reached? How specific should goals be?

Here are two examples of counseling goals. The counselor and client might agree to:

a. Help the client develop more fully his self-actualizing potential, or

b. Increase the frequency of positive self-statements emitted by the client.

Both of these could be considered good counseling outcomes. They might be so closely related as to be the same in terms of outcomes. To the client, developing self-actualizing potential is a more general and overall objective. It may hold more meaning or attraction for him. To the counselor, developing self-actualizing potential may be a composite of more specific goals. Stated a little differently, self-actualizing is a hypothetical state that cannot be observed. It can only be inferred through certain visible or audible behaviors of the client. Using this goal, the counselor has no way of knowing the types of activity the client will enter into as he proceeds toward attaining the goal. As a result, the counselor knows very little about what he should be doing in the relationship, and the client has no way of assessing his progress.

Consequently, the first goal (a) is not as satisfactory in that it does not provide the counselor with guidelines for conducting the helping relationship.

---

1. Hypothetical goals can be inferred only through certain (a)

_____ **or (b)** _____ **behaviors.**

TYPES OF GOALS

The counselor uses two types of goals or objectives, *process* goals and *outcome* goals. Process goals are related to the establishment of therapeutic conditions necessary for client change. These are general goals such as establishing rapport with the client, providing a non-threatening setting, and possessing and communicating accurate empathy and unconditional regard. They can be generalized to all client relationships and can be considered universal goals. Process goals are the primary responsibility of the counselor; he cannot expect the client to help him establish and communicate something such as unconditional regard.

Objectives such as "establishing rapport" are still in a hypothetical state. To define such goals more specifically, we must identify counselor behaviors that are likely to occur simultaneously. For example, when a good rapport is being established, should the counselor smile? Should he begin talking about serious or light matters? Should he take rigid or tentative positions on topics?

The answers to Item 1 are (a) **visible** and (b) **audible**.

---

2. Using what you have learned in previous chapters, make a list of counselor behaviors you think would be related to the hypothetical construct "Accurate Empathy." Begin with:

    1. The counselor listens to the client without interrupting him.

    2. _____

    3. _____

Compare your list with the lists of two other persons.

Outcome Goals

Unlike *process* goals, *outcome* goals will be different for each client. They are the goals directly related to the client's reasons for seeking counseling. Outcome goals can be vague and imprecise, or specific and precise. Regardless of their form, they must be goals to which the client can relate and accept as his own. Consequently, outcome goals become *shared* goals, goals which both the counselor and client agree to work toward achieving.

3. Outcomes goals are objectives which the counselor and client

    _____.

When outcome goals are stated precisely, both the counselor and the client have a better understanding of what is to be accomplished. This better understanding permits them to work more directly with the client's problems or concerns, and reduces tangential efforts. As an example, a student counselor was seeing a client whose problem was the friction building up between her and her brother over use of the family car. A vague goal could have been:

> To develop a greater understanding of her feelings, her brother's feelings, and their relationship.

In fact the counselor and client established a much more specific goal:

> To learn how to schedule the use of the family car to avoid conflicts which are friction-producing.

Equally important are the benefits the counselor realizes in working with specific behavioral goals. He is able to enlist the client's cooperation more directly since the client is more likely to understand what is to be done. In addition, the counselor is in a better position to select techniques and strategies when he has specific objectives. Finally, both client and counselor are in a better position to recognize progress, a rewarding experience in its own right.

EXERCISE: GOAL SETTING

Tom is a junior in college. He is bright, personable, but a little bit shy. He came to counseling with the problem of relating to girls. Specifically, he believes that there is some flaw in his personality that "turns girls off." His reasons for thinking this grow out of his experience with dating. He reports that girls go out with him once or twice and then don't accept any more dates. He admits to getting discouraged when he calls a girl for a date and she says she already has a commitment. If this happens twice, he never calls the girl again, assuming that she doesn't want to date him.

Identify two or three goals which you think might be appropriate in working with Tom, given that you know very little about him.

1. _____

    _____

2. _____

    _____

3. _____

    _____

Are your goals specific or vague? How would you and Tom know when you had achieved these goals? Are your goals *process* or *outcome* goals? If they are process goals, would you need to involve Tom in their establishment? If they are outcome goals, how would achieving them affect Tom's dating problem?

The correct answer to Item 3 is **share** or **agree upon.**

CLIENT PARTICIPATION
IN GOAL SETTING

Often, the discussion of goal setting is construed to mean that the counselor listens to the client, makes a mental assessment of the problem, and prescribes a solution or goal. In fact, such a procedure is doomed to failure. The nature of counseling is such that the client must be involved in the establishment of goals. Otherwise, his participation is directionless at best, and interferes with counseling at worst. An example will illustrate this better. A beginning counselor was seeing a client who was overweight, self-conscious about her appearance, reluctant to enter into social relationships with others because of this self-consciousness, and very lonely. Realizing that the problem of being overweight was an important factor, the counselor informed the client that one goal would be for the client to lose three to four pounds per week, under a medical doctor's supervision. With this, the client became highly defensive, and rejected the counselor's goal, saying: "You sound just like my mother."

Such goal setting is highly personal. It requires total effort on the client's part. Therefore, it must be a goal identified by the client as important enough to make sacrifices to achieve. The counselor should have moved more slowly, permitting the client to identify for herself the significance of her overweight, and then identify, together, the weight-reducing goal.

CLIENT RESISTANCE
TO GOAL SETTING

Upon completing a counseling session with her client, a counselor said, "This was the fourth interview, and I still cannot get him to talk about goals." Occasionally, clients resist the notion of goal setting. When this happens, the counselor must deal with the question, "Why is the client resisting?"

In working with the resistant client, we shall assume that behavior is purposeful. That is, what the client does or avoids doing achieves some desirable result for the client. Consequently, we may find that the client who resists setting goals may be protecting the behavior which is in need of modification because he sees that behavior as doing something desirable for him also. An example is the chronic smoker. While he may recognize the negative consequences of smoking, he also clings to the habit, believing that it helps him through tense situations, helps him relax, helps him appreciate a good meal, etc.

It becomes the counselor's task to get the client to identify what he gains from his current behavior. In so doing, the client and counselor may determine whether or not that gain or outcome can be achieved in more desirable ways. For example, if a student throws paper airplanes out of the school window his purpose may be to achieve attention from his peers. Gaining attention may be a desirable outcome. It is the method which is the problem. Therefore, the counselor and client may consider more appropriate means for gaining increased attention other than throwing airplanes out of the school window.

---

4. Precise goals permit the client to recognize _____ **more easily.**

Krumboltz and Thoresen [1] have noted that rarely does a client begin by requesting assistance in achieving specific behavior changes. Instead of saying: "I want to be able to talk to teachers without getting nervous," he is likely to say: "I am shy." In other words, he describes a characteristic about himself rather than the ways in which the characteristic is experienced. It then becomes the counselor's job to help the client describe the ways in which he would like to act differently when he is feeling shy.

Answer to Item 4 is **progress, change,** or **improvement.**

---

5. The counselor must help the client describe his problem in terms

of _____ **which he would like to change.**

TRANSLATING COMPLAINTS
INTO OBJECTIVES

Taking non-specific complaints and translating them into specific objectives is no easy task for the counselor. He must understand the nature of the client's problem and the conditions under which it occurs be-

[1] J. D. Krumboltz and C. E. Thoresen, *Behavioral Counseling, Cases and Techniques* (New York: Holt, Rinehart & Winston, 1969), pp. 7–8.

fore the translation can begin. Even then there are difficulties. Krumboltz and Thoresen list seven stumbling blocks that counselors may face as they attempt to define behavioral goals:

1. The client views his problem as someone else's behavior.
2. The client expresses the problem as a *feeling*.
3. The problem is the absence of a goal.
4. The problem is that a desired behavior is undesirable.
5. The problem is that the client does not know his behavior is inappropriate.
6. The problem is a choice conflict.
7. The problem is a vested interest in not identifying any problem.[2]

Answer to Item 5 is **behavior.**

---

6. In order to establish behavioral objectives the counselor must

understand the (a) _____ of the client's prob-

lems and the (b) _____ under which they occur.

What can you as a counselor expect of yourself and your clients in terms of setting specific goals? First, the goals that are set can never be more specific than your understanding and the client's understanding of the problem. This means that at the outset of counseling, goals are likely to be non-specific and non-behavioral. *But non-specific goals are better than no goals at all.*

Krumboltz describes these non-specific or general goals as *intermediate* mental states, but he emphasizes that one cannot assume that such goals will "free up" the client to change his overt behavior.[3] The point is that although intermediate goals may be necessary at the outset of counseling or until the counselor has some specific knowledge of the client, such goals must be viewed as temporary. At the earliest possible time the counselor and client must strive to identify more specific and behavioral goals.

---

[2] *Ibid.,* pp. 9–18.
[3] J. D. Krumboltz, "Behavioral Goals for Counseling," *Journal of Counseling Psychology,* 13 (1966), p. 153.

Answers to Item 6 are (a) **nature** and (b) **conditions.**

---

7. As you and your client become more understanding of his prob-

lems, you will be able to identify more specific or _____

_____ goals.

There are various types of outcome goals. Osipow and Walsh [4] have identified three classes: goals dealing with the client's interpersonal effectiveness, goals dealing with his efficiency in his work, and subjective evaluations of his overall competence. Krumboltz,[5] using a different frame of reference has classified behavioral goals as altering maladaptive behavior, learning the decision-making process, and preventing problems.

Answer to Item **7** is **behavioral.**

As you and your client explore the nature of a particular problem, the type of goal(s) appropriate to the problem should become increasingly clear. This clarification will permit you and the client to move in the direction of identifying specific behaviors which, if changed, would alter the problem in a positive way. This process of examining and understanding the problem becomes an initial goal. It might be stated:

Goal 1: To identify the conditions surrounding the occurrence of the problem.

Goal 2: To identify situational events that can be modified to produce different consequences for the client.

Through your questions and guidance, the client must learn to look at his problem in a systematic and analytic way. For example, let us assume that a client, Nancy, has come to you for counseling. She describes her problem as a depressed state in which she can see no meaning in what she is doing, has no sense of where she is going in her life, and in general, lacks a purpose in life. Such a problem might be described as an

---

[4] S. H. Osipow and W. B. Walsh, *Strategies in Counseling for Behavior Change* (New York: Appleton-Century-Crofts, 1970), p. 30.
[5] Krumboltz, "Behavioral Goals," pp. 23–25.

existential crisis, a lack of self-awareness, an inability to integrate one's experiences into one's perceptions of reality. None of these classifications of the problem enhances its understanding. In fact, all too little is known about the problem to classify it at this time.

PINNING DOWN THE PROBLEM

There are a number of things that need to be known about Nancy and her depressed state. Many of the missing pieces of information can be drawn out with a few questions. Some questions relevant to Nancy's depression would be:

1. Is this a constant depressed state or do you move in and out of it?
2. If it is not a constant depressed state, what are the conditions surrounding its occurrence? Where are you when you start feeling depressed? Are you with someone else? If so, who? Is it day, evening, or night? Are you doing something or are you inactive?
3. When was the last time you felt depressed? How long did it last? Did you emerge from your depression gradually or suddenly? Was anyone with you as you emerged from the depression? Where were you? What were you doing?

These questions are not a comprehensive list. They will give you an idea of what you and the client are attempting to establish. The underlying assumption is that the client's feelings cannot be isolated from his environment. Feelings and environment are continually interacting.

As you and Nancy probe the facets of her problems, increasing your understanding of the situational components, you will be able to identify events or conditions that elicit depressive reactions. Together you can consider to what extent these situational components *can* be modified, and when modified, produce *different consequences* for Nancy.

At this point an outline of goals can be constructed. We refer to an outline because the major headings are the original complaints, and the sub-headings are the behavioral goals related to those complaints. For example:

I. Identify meaning or significance in the activities in which Nancy engages. (Nancy's complaint: She sees no meaning in what she is doing.)
   A. To learn how to identify the social significance inherent in activities.
   B. To increase Nancy's positive responses to these activities.

    C. To reduce the effect unpleasant activities have upon Nancy's self-evaluative processes.

    D. To establish an effective set of activities which will intervene when Nancy begins feeling depressed about her activities (e.g., leave the apartment, do some shopping, go out to a concert).

  II. To help Nancy develop a sense of direction or purpose in her life. (Nancy's complaint: She has no sense of where she is going in her life.)

Perhaps you can complete the goal outline for the second major objective, "Helping Nancy develop a sense of direction or purpose." You might begin by establishing the criteria Nancy would consider important. Who are some of the people who, to Nancy, appear to have this sense of direction? What do these people do that gives Nancy this impression or feeling? From this kind of information and using your own imagination, construct the specific types of goals which would implement this second objective.

Notice how the objectives or goals which are established have two necessary conditions:

1. They begin as overall goals that are directly related to the client's specific or general complaints or descriptions of his problems, and

2. Specific, behaviorally observable sub-goals are established which, if achieved, permit the realization of the overall goal.

Thus, goal-setting moves from general to specific goals; the specific goals are directly related to the general goal, and the general goal is a reflection of the problems presented to the counselor.

RECOMMENDED READINGS

KRUMBOLTZ, J. D., "Behavioral Goals for Counseling," *Journal of Counseling Psychology,* 13 (1966), 153–59.

Krumboltz presents the criteria that should be met in setting counseling goals, types of behavioral goals, and the relationship between goal-setting and progress in counseling.

————, and THORESEN, C. E., *Behavorial Counseling: Cases and Techniques.* New York: Holt, Rinehart and Winston, 1969.

The authors provide in their introduction to Part I (pp. 7–18) an excellent discussion of helping the client with problem identification.

OSIPOW, S. H. and WALSH, W. B., *Strategies in Counseling for Behavior Change.* New York: Appleton-Century-Crofts, 1970.

Osipow and Walsh discuss "Assessment" (Chapter 2) and compare different approaches to the diagnosis of client problems and the process of setting behavioral goals.

7

Responding to
Client
Cognitive Contents

The counselor responds to the client in many ways, both verbally and nonverbally. Since your responses will have an impact on the client and the topics he discusses, it is necessary to be aware of the effect your responses will have. One very important effect deals with the changing pattern of the client's verbal behavior. As the verbal interaction and communication begin, topics arise; some topics are developed, some are modified and some are diverted into new topics. As an active participant in the counseling process, your responses will influence the direction of topic development in ways such as choosing from among the topics which is to be discussed and the length of time allotted to the topic.

The purpose of this chapter is to acquaint you with and give you practice in recognizing different kinds of cognitive content, and in developing appropriate counselor responses for use with cognitive content. Responding to client content suggests alternatives and conscious choices which you will have to make in the interview. Then, when one choice has been made, the effect of that choice will become the basis for further alternatives. The following example will illustrate the types of choices you, the counselor, will be making. Suppose your client says:

> Client: "I've known what this operation would do to my plans for a long time."

Your choices for responding are several. You could (1) paraphrase the client's remark; (2) accent the word "operation" or the words "your plans"; (3) ask the question "what will it do?"; (4) say "mm-hmm" or (5) present an ability potential type of response, "you are able to anticipate the consequences of the operation."

Obviously, these five stimuli will produce different responses from the client. The client may proceed to talk about the operation, about his plans, or about how he "anticipates" events, etc. In any case, your response would shape or mold the topic development, and as a result, influence the future matters the client discusses.

---

1. The counselor, as an active participant in the counseling process, uses responses which exert influence on _____ _____ **(two words).**

In this chapter you will be working with content choices of a cognitive nature, as opposed to affective or feeling-type choices. In other words, the emphasis now is on your recognition and demonstrated ability to identify and respond to client thoughts or ideas dealing with *events, people,* or *things.*

The correct answer to Item 1 is **topic development** or **topic direction.** If this seems unclear, re-read page 52.

---

2. The counselor's ability to modify topics of cognitive nature includes those thoughts dealing with (a) _____,

(b) _____, **and (c)** _____.

RECOGNIZING ALTERNATIVES

Each communication of the client presents alternatives to the counselor in terms of content to which he may respond. How you respond to one alternative shapes the next remark of the client. The counselor's task is to identify accurately the kinds of content presented by the client and the alternatives to which you as the counselor can respond.

The correct answers to Item 2 are (a) **events,** (b) **people,** and (c) **things.** See page 52 for further information.

---

3. The counselor must identify the content and (a) _____

or (b) _____ **presented in the client's communication.**

RESPONDING TO ALTERNATIVES

The process of selecting alternatives can best be illustrated by excerpts from actual interviews:

Client: "I like this type of a set-up where you can talk directly to people and talk with them. Uh, I don't like big crowds where I don't know anybody and they don't know me."

Counselor: "You're uncomfortable in big crowds."

In this example, the client's response contained two basic communications: (a) I like to talk directly to people and (b) I don't like big crowds in which individuals get lost.

The counselor chose to respond to the second communication in the client's response. Had he responded by saying "You prefer situations which permit you to get to know people," the topic focus would have been upon getting to know people and the necessary conditions for this. As it was, his response led to a topic focus related to the ambiguity of not knowing people. This does not necessarily mean that one response was more appropriate than the other; it is used only to point out the available alternatives.

The correct answers to Item 3 are **alternatives** and **choices**.
Look back to page 52 if necessary.

4. The counselor is frequently faced with the choice of topics. By his responding with interest to one topic as opposed to another,

he is _____ one topic over the other.

A study of counseling typescripts suggests that when the counselor has alternative communications to which he may respond, his tendency is to respond to the final component of the response. Perhaps this is because of the immediacy of the final part of the response, but if so, this is a poor criterion. It is more logical that the counselor respond to the part of the client's communication that has greatest bearing on the client's concern and is therefore most important.

The counselor may also be tempted to respond to that portion of the client's communication in which he personally is most interested. In this case the interview tends to center around those topics that the counselor may identify with or be dealing with himself. Again, the counselor must insure that his choice of alternative topics reflects a decision about the client's needs rather than his own.

The correct answer to Item 4 is **reinforcing** or **rewarding**. If this answer was not apparent, you might review the material in the chapter on counselor reinforcing behavior, specifically that part on the effects of the counselor's attentiveness.

EXERCISES

A. To give you practice in identifying topic alternatives, read carefully the following client statements. Then identify and list all the different topics that exist in each client response.

1. "They have, but I don't know just exactly how it does work, but you can sign up to take weekend trips in connection with the Air Force. It would be like duty because you have to qualify for it and you can travel all over the U.S."
   The different topics are:

a. _____

_____

b. _____

_____

c. _____

_____

d. _____

_____

e. _____

_____

2. "And I thought it was great. And I realize that most people have a bad opinion of women in the service but, uh, they shouldn't really, because a woman is going to be what she is, no matter where she is."

a. _____

_____

b. _____

_____

c. _____

_____

d. _____

_____

The correct answers to the exercises above are:

1. a. *I don't know just exactly how it does work.*
   b. *You can sign up to take weekend trips in connection with the Air Force.*

    c. *It would be like duty.*
    d. *You have to qualify for it.*
    e. *You can travel all over the U.S.*

2. a. *I thought it was great.*
    b. *I realize that most people have a bad opinion of women in the service.*
    c. *They shouldn't really.*
    d. *A woman is going to be what she is no matter where she is.*

B. To give further practice in identifying *cognitive* contents, such as thoughts or ideas pertaining to events, people, or things, read carefully the following client statements. Then identify and list the different *cognitive* topics within each client response.

1. "I'm thinking about either going to grad school or getting a job—whichever would be better experience is what I'll do."
   The different cognitive content topics are:

   a. _____

   _____

   b. _____

   _____

   c. _____

   _____

2. "People can say whatever they want about it, but as far as I'm concerned, my place as a woman is in the home and it will not change."
   The different cognitive content topics are:

   a. _____

   _____

   b. _____

   _____

   c. _____

   _____

The correct answers to the exercises given above are:

1. a. *I'm thinking about going to grad school.*
   b. *I'm also thinking about getting a job.*
   c. *I'll do whatever provides the best experience.*

2. a. *People can say whatever they want to about a woman's place.*
   b. *I think my place as a woman is in the home.*
   c. *My opinion about this will not change.*

TYPES OF DISCRIMINATING STIMULI

There are several types of responses you can use as stimuli to focus upon and elicit specific content expressed in the client's communication. The stimuli presented here will be ones that can be used specifically to respond to cognitive content of the client's communication; that is, ideas that deal with *events, people,* and *things.*

Although these are not the only possible ones, four stimulus discriminators (SD) will be identified here for this purpose: silence, minimal verbal activity, restatement, and probe. Emphasis will be directed toward the latter two.

---

5. **There are a variety of counselor responses that can be used in response to specific content in clients' communications. Four stimuli that are useful discriminators for cognitive content are**

   silence, minimal verbal activity, (a) _____,

   and the (b) _____.

The use of silence and minimal verbal stimuli has already been noted (Chapters Three and Four). Their use as discriminators will be presented here briefly.

Silence

Silence affects the course of topic development as a discriminative stimulus by indicating that the counselor does not want to select or direct the topic at the given time it is used. Although the use of silence gives the counselor much less control over the direction topic development takes, it serves to increase the power of other types of responses. Thus, after you have remained silent for several moments, your next verbal response will be more valued by the client and, as a result, will have more influence in shaping the direction of topic development.

The correct answers to Item 5 are (a) **restatement** and the (b) **probe**. Go back to page 57 for review.

---

6. **Silence increases the discriminative power of other types of counselor responses. At the same time, silence permits much**

   less _____ over topic development.

Minimal Verbal Activity

Minimal verbal stimuli are those verbalizations and vocalizations that people use when they are listening to someone else. The most common are "mm-hmm," "mmm," "yes," "oh," "I see," etc. They are unobtrusive utterances but have a significant reinforcing value. That is to say, when an utterance such as "mm-hmm" is used consistently following a particular topic or word, the future occurrence of that particular topic or word increases.

The correct answer to Item 6 is **control** or **influence.**

---

7. **If a particular verbalization or vocalization is a good reinforcer, when it is used following a specific topic or idea, the probability of that same topic or word being emitted in the future**

   _____.

Restatements

The restatement is the repetition of all or a selected portion of the client's previous communication, and neither adds nor detracts from the basic communication. It confirms for the client that the counselor has heard his communication. Operationally, the restatement may be defined as a simple, compound, complex, or fragmentary sentence emitted to mirror the client's previous communication. It is dependent in its grammatical structure upon the grammatical structure of the client's previous response. The restatement can be used effectively so long as it is interspersed with other types of counselor responses. Otherwise, it can produce a "parrot-like" effect that has a negatively reinforcing effect upon clients.

The correct answer to Item 7 is **increases** or **is greater.** Check back to page 58 if you don't understand this.

---

8. **The restatement is a** _____**of all or part of the client's previous communication.**

Some examples of restatements will help you understand this particular discriminative stimulus.

Client: "I'm hoping to get a good job this summer."
Counselor: "You're hoping to get a good job." (RESTATEMENT)
Client: "It doesn't look like we'll get a vacation this summer."
Counselor: "No vacation this summer." (RESTATEMENT)
Client: "I like people but I sure get tired of them."
Counselor: "You like people but you also get tired of them." (RESTATEMENT)

Now, try your hand with a few restatements:

Client: "This has been a really rough year for me."

You: "_____."

Client: "Probably the worst class I have is literature."

You: "_____."

DISCUSS YOUR RESPONSES WITH SOMEONE.

The correct answer to Item 8 is **repetition** or **replication.**
See page 58 about this answer.

---

9. When you restate the client's communication, it tends to _____

_____ to the client that you have heard him.

Probes

The probe is a question that requires more than a minimal one-word answer by the client. It is introduced with either *what, where, when,* or *how*. You will find that it is very difficult to ask questions that clearly place the focus upon your client. Typically, when you, the counselor, start asking questions, the client will give a minimal answer and then wait for the next question. In other words, the client has not assumed responsibility for the content of the interview. The purpose of the probe is to prevent the client from answering questions with a "yes" or "no" response.

Some examples of probes include the following:

"What do you like about it?" "What is keeping you from doing it?" "How do you feel about it?" "How is it helping you?" "When do you feel that way?" "Where does that occur for you?"

A probe can easily be overused in an interview. A beginning counselor often tends to bombard initial clients with questions. Extensive use of the probe in subsequent interviews can, however, give a "ping-pong" effect; the counselor asks, the client answers and so on.

Try a few probes out for yourself.

Client: "It's hard to admit, but I really have wondered whether college is for me."

You: "_____"

Client: "I've gotten to the point where I can't do anything I'm supposed to do."

You: "_____"

DISCUSS YOUR RESPONSES WITH SOMEONE.

The correct answer to Item 9 is **confirm** or **convey**.
Refer back to page 59 if needed.

10. The probe is a question that requires a process-type of answer,

as opposed to a _____ response.

The following exercises will give you practice in using the restatement and the probe. Read each client statement and then respond with the type of response indicated in parentheses:

1. Client: "Yes, I think that the best way to learn a language is to actually live with the people and learn it that way. Um, the first year that I was going back to Germany, I didn't learn very much at all."

    You: (RESTATEMENT) "_____

    _____."

2. Client: "I'd like to know the language, but still I can't carry on a conversation because it isn't used that much in my classes."

    You: (PROBE) "_____

    _____."

3. Client: "I wanted to go back to school mostly because of the fact that I thought that there would be someone to lead because I just don't know which direction to go sometimes for a few things."

    You: (RESTATEMENT) "_____

    _____."

4. Client: "Well, I know you're supposed to study every night, which I don't do, but I'm not the only one who hasn't studied this semester. A lot of other kids have lost interest too."

    You: (PROBE) "_____

    _____."

DISCUSS YOUR RESPONSES WITH SOMEONE.

The correct answer to Item 10 is **minimal** or **short.**
Look over the section on page 60.

DISCRIMINATION AND
SELECTIVE REINFORCEMENT

The emphasis in this chapter has been on the selective reinforcement of some client messages as opposed to others. When the client presents you with a multiple message, you can respond to all the messages or to only part of them. If you respond to only part of the client's messages, that part to which you don't respond will probably be dropped by the client in future communications. Using your responses to the client in the exercise on the previous page, write what you think would be the client's following response to what you said. For example, with response 1, if you had said "When were you in Germany?", the client might have responded "I was there from 1969 through 1971."

1. Your response was: "_____

_____."

Client's next response: "_____

_____."

2. Your response was: "_____

_____."

Client's next response: "_____

_____."

3. Your response was: "_____

_____."

Client's next response: "_____

_____."

4. Discuss with another person how your stimulus caused the client to respond in one way rather than another. Did your stimulus discriminate between the various topics the client presented?

With your triad, complete the following exercise:

1. One of you, designated as the speaker, should share a thought or idea with the respondent.
2. The respondent's task is to respond *only* to cognitive topics using only the four responses covered in the chapter: silence, minimal verbal activity, restatement, and probe.
3. The observer will use the Observer Rating Chart (page 64) to keep track of the number and kinds of responses given. This feedback should then be given to the respondent.
4. After interacting in one triad for approximately ten minutes, reverse the roles.

OBSERVER RATING CHART

Type of Counselor Response

Counselor Response	Silence	Minimal Verbal	Restatement	Probe	Other
1.					
2.					
3.					
4.					
5.					
6.					
7.					
8.					
9.					
10.					

11.					
12.					
13.					
14.					
15.					
16.					
17.					
18.					

8

Responding to Client Affective Contents

What are some of the ways you communicate how you feel? When you're "down in the dumps," how does your voice sound? When you're angry, what is your face like, your mouth, your eyes, your jaw? When you're afraid, what are some of the expressions you use to communicate this feeling? Human beings have many ways of communicating their internal states. The set jaw often is associated with determination. The glaring eyes speak for anger, even in the small child. The trembling voice, the soft voice, the downcast eyes, all these have their meanings.

Clients use all of the verbal and nonverbal modes to tell the counselor of their problems. The emotions that accompany the narrative enrich and modify the message. They give the counselor the events of the client's world *and* the client's reactions to those events. These cues are not always easy to read. Clenched teeth can mean more than one thing. The trembling voice only suggests the presence of an intense emotion. A part of being a counselor is putting together the pieces or cues of the client's message in such a way that you can make reasonably good guesses about the underlying emotion.

As Chapter Seven indicated, the client's communication presents alternatives. In addition to alternative cognitive topics, you will find that you are faced with choices between cognitive topics and affective topics. This chapter focuses upon the affective message, how to recognize it, and how to reinforce its exploration by the client.

---

1. The factual details of the client's story describe the events of

his world and the accompanying emotions describe his _____

_____ to those events.

As a brief review, those client communications that deal primarily with people, events, or objects may be described as *cognitive* details. Communications that reflect feelings or emotions usually are described as *affective* details. Many messages contain both cognitive and affective components. When this occurs, the affective message may not be obvious in the words of the client. Instead, the feelings may be expressed through nonverbal modes, such as vocal pitch, rapidity of speech, bodily positions and/or gestures, etc.

The correct answer to Item 1 is **reaction** or **response**.

VERBAL AND NONVERBAL CUES
ASSOCIATED WITH EMOTIONS

You may have wondered how you can identify another person's feelings. Although you cannot feel the client's feelings, you can infer what his feelings are and experience very similar feelings. That is to say, you may be able to know what it is like to feel a certain way. How do you do this? You can draw from your own emotional experiences and know that you, too, have experienced pain, anger, joy, and remember how that felt. You must first recognize the feeling in your client before you can reproduce a similar feeling in yourself.

To do this you may need to become more aware of and sensitive to certain *verbal* and *nonverbal* cues that are elements of the client's communication. Some of these cues are referred to as "leakage" [1] since they

[1] P. Ekman and W. V. Friesen, "Nonverbal Leakage and Clues to Deception," *Psychiatry,* 32 (1969), 88–105.

communicate messages the client did not deliberately intend to have communicated. Other cues, primarily verbal, are more deliberately intended and are more easily recognized and identified.

In the case of affective leakage, it is important to account for the inferences you may draw. For example, when you say "The client seems happy," this is an inference. If you say instead, "The client is smiling and that may mean that he is happy," then you have accounted for your inference.

---

2. One way to infer a client's feeling state is to draw on your own emotional experiences; another very important way is to become sensitized to _____ and nonverbal elements of the client's communication.

The total impact of a client's message includes both verbal and nonverbal elements. The verbal impact means that there are certain nouns, adjectives, adverbs, and verbs that express the client's feelings about something or someone. For example:

"I am really *worried* about school."

The verbal element associated with the client's feelings in this example is the word "worried." These kinds of words can be called *affect* words. They express some feeling that the client possesses. If an adverb such as *really* or *very* precedes the affect word, this indicates an even stronger intensity of emotion.

EXERCISE: IDENTIFICATION BEHAVIOR

Pick a partner. Interact for about five minutes. Then each of you should describe, in turn, your partner, using the phrase:

"I'm observing that you are _____."

Be sure to describe what you *see,* not how you think the other person feels.

Answer to Item 2 is **verbal.**

---

3. Underline the affect words in the following statements:
   "It really hurt when she said that."
   "I guess I'm afraid to try harder."

Nonverbal Cues to Affect

Nonverbal cues can be seen from such elements of the client's communication as head and facial movement, position of body, quick movements and gestures, and voice quality. Although no single nonverbal cue can be interpreted accurately alone, each does have meaning as part of a larger pattern or gestalt. Thus there are relationships between nonverbal and verbal aspects of speech. In addition to the relationship between nonverbal and verbal parts of the message, nonverbal cues may also communicate specific information about the relationship of the people involved in the communicative process, in this case, the counselor and client. Nonverbal cues differentially convey information about the *nature* and *intensity* of emotions, sometimes more accurately than verbal cues. The *nature* of the emotion is communicated nonverbally primarily by *head* cues, the *intensity* of an emotion is communicated both by *head* cues and *body* cues.[2]

Answers to Item 3 are **really hurt** and **afraid.**

4. Both verbal and nonverbal cues convey information about the nature and intensity of an emotion. For nonverbal cues, the

_____ **of an emotion is communicated both by head and body cues.**

Types of Affective Messages

Although there are many different kinds of feelings, most feelings that we identify by words fit into one of three areas: affection, anger, or

[2] P. Ekman and W. Friesen, "Head and Body Cues in the Judgment of Emotion: A Reformulation," *Perceptual and Motor Skills,* 24 (1967), 711–24.

fear. Feelings of affection reflect positive or good feelings about oneself and others, and indicate positive feelings about interpersonal relationships. Many of them can be identified by certain affect words. There are several subcategories of affect words used to express positive feelings about oneself and others. These subcategories include: *enjoyment, competence, love, happiness,* and *hope.*

Answer to Item 4 is **intensity.**

---

5. Most feelings can be classified into three general categories:

(a) _____, **(b)** _____ **and (c)** _____

_____ .

AFFECTION.   Affect word cues that communicate the general feeling of affection may be subclassified into five general areas. Some examples of these word cues [3] are:

Enjoyment	*Competence*	*Love*	*Happiness*	*Hope*
beautiful	able	close	cheerful	luck
enjoy	can	friendly	content	optimism
good	fulfill	love	delighted	try
nice	great	like	excited	guess
pretty	wonderful	need	happy	wish
satisfy	smart	care	laugh(ed)	want
terrific	respect	want	thrill	
tremendous	worth	choose	dig	

You can continue to add to this list of affect words related to affection. Can you begin to get the feeling for the message implicit in the usage of words such as these?

Answers to Item 5 are (a) **anger,** (b) **fear,** and (c) **affection.**

---

[3] Word lists for affection, fear, and anger are taken, in part, from T. J. Crowley, "The Conditionability of Positive and Negative Self-reference Emotional Affect Statements in a Counseling-type Interview" (Doctoral dissertation, The University of Massachusetts, 1970).

6. Affect word cues that suggest enjoyment or attraction would be classified as _____.

Certain nonverbal cues often occur simultaneously with affection word cues. The most obvious of these cues are facial ones. The corners of the mouth may turn up to produce the hint of a smile. The eyes may widen slightly. "Worry" wrinkles disappear. Often there is an absence of body tension. The arms and hands may be moved in an open-palm gesture of acceptance, or the communicator may reach out and touch the object of the affection message lightly. When the client is describing feelings about an object or event, there may be increased animation of the face and hands.

Answer to Item 6 is **affection.**

7. Facial expressions that characteristically accompany expression of affection cues include a slight (a) _____ **and widening of the (b)** _____.

ANGER.   Anger represents an obstruction to be relieved or removed in some way. Different kinds of stimuli often elicit anger. One such stimulus is frustration. Another is *threat* or *fear*. Conditions such as competition, jealousy, and thwarted aspirations can become threats that elicit angry responses. Anger often represents *negative* feelings about oneself and/or others. Often fear is concealed by an outburst of anger. In such cases the anger becomes a defensive reaction because the person does not feel safe enough to express his fear. Anger is also a cover-up for hurt. Beneath strong aggressive outbursts are often deep feelings of vulnerability and pain.

Answers to Item 7 are (a) **smile** and (b) **eyes.**

8. Two stimuli that are capable of eliciting anger are

(a) _____ and (b) _____.

Verbal cues which suggest *anger* may be classified into four general categories. These are:

Attack	Grimness	Defensiveness	Quarrelsome
argue	dislike	against	angry
attack	hate	protect	fight
compete	nasty	resent	quarrel
criticize	disgust	guard	argue
fight	surly	prepared	take issue
hit	serious		reject
hurt			(don't) agree
offend			

Add to this list of affect words which suggest *anger*. Remember that anger covers a broad group of feelings and can be expressed in many ways.

Answers to Item 8 are (a) **frustration** and (b) **fear** or (a) **hurt** and (b) **threat**.

9. The word "disgusting" would fall into the general category of

(a) _____ while the word "enjoy" would fall

into the category of (b) _____.

With the expression of anger, the body position may become rigid and tense or it may be characterized by gross changes in body position or movement if the client is expressing direct dislike of the counselor or someone else in the room.[4] Sometimes anger toward another person or the self may be expressed by "hitting," which consists of "fault-finding" or petty remarks directed at the object of the anger. For example, in counseling a couple with marital problems, one partner may express this sort of anger by continual verbal attacks on the other person or by incessant

---

[4] A. Mehrabrian, "Communication Without Words," *Psychology Today,* 2 (1968), 53–55.

remarks of dissatisfaction with the partner. "Hitting" can also be expressed through nonverbal cues such as finger drumming or foot tapping.

Answers to Item 9 are (a) **anger** and (b) **affection.**

---

10. **Anger can be expressed indirectly or directly. An indirect expression of anger would be through the body position which**

   may become (a) _____ or (b) _____.

There are certain vocal qualities also associated with anger. Many times the voice will become much *louder* as the person becomes more rigid in what he is saying; if the anger is very intense, the person may even shout. In some instances of intense anger, the feeling may be accompanied by *tears*.

Many times the expression of anger will cause vocal pitch to become *higher*. With some people, however, the vocal pitch actually is lowered, becoming more *controlled* and *measured*. This usually means that the person experiencing the anger is attempting to maintain a level of control over his feelings.

Answers to Item 10 are (a) **rigid** and (b) **tense.**

---

11. **The voice of an angry person often becomes (a) _____**

   as the vocal pitch becomes (b) _____.

FEAR.   Fear represents a person's reaction to some kind of danger to be avoided. Often this reaction is a withdrawal from a painful or stressful situation, from one's self, or from other people and relationships. As such, the person experiencing the emotions of fear may also be *isolated* and *sad* or *depressed*. Fear can also be described as a *negative* set of feelings about something or someone that results in a need to protect oneself.

Answers to Item 11 are (a) **louder** and (b) **higher.**

Verbal cues that suggest fear may be classified into five general categories. These are:

Fear	Doubt	Sadness	Pain	Avoidance
anxious	failure	alone	awful	flee
bothers	flunk	depressed	hurts	run from
concerns	undecided	dismay	intense	escape
lonely	mediocre	disillusion	unpleasant	cut out
nervous	moody	discouraged	uncomfortable	forget
scare	puzzled	sad	aches	
tense	stupid	tired	torn	
upset	unsure	unhappy		
		weary		

Add to this list of affect words suggesting *fear*. Remember that fear is a broad category of feelings and can be expressed in many ways.

FEAR AND NONVERBAL CUES.   There are several facial cues associated with fear. The mouth may hang wide open as in shock or startledness; the eyes may also dilate. Fear may cause a furrow to appear between the eyebrows. Fear of the counselor or of the topic at hand may be reflected by the client's *avoidance* of *direct eye contact*.

Body positions and movements are also associated with the expression of fear. At first the person experiencing fear may appear to be *still* in body position or may *draw back*. However, after this initial period, body movement usually becomes greater as anxiety increases. Body movements may be *jerky* and *trembling*. Although parts of the body may *shake,* often the hands are tightly *clasped* as if giving protection. Tension may also be indicated through actions such as leg swinging, foot tapping, or playing with a ring or piece of jewelry.

---

12. The body position of a person experiencing fear may at first

be (a) _____ **but body movement increases as**

(b) _____ **increases.**

FEAR AND VERBAL CUES.   Voice qualities are also indicators of the level of anxiety the client is experiencing. As the level of anxiety increases the breathing rate becomes *faster* and breathing becomes more *shallow*. Also, as anxiety and tension increase, the number of speech disturbances *increases*. This yields a greater number of cues, such as errors, repetitions, stutterings, and omissions of parts of words or sentences.[3] The rate of speech also increases as anxiety mounts, so an anxious person may speak at a faster than usual rate. The intonation of a depressed person or one in the grip of fear is also a departure from the normal intonation. The voice quality may become more *subdued* with less inflection so that the voice takes on more of a *monotonal* quality.

Answers to Item 12 are (a) **still** or **stiff** and (b) **anxiety.**

In summary, the three main *affect* areas are those of *affection, anger,* and *fear.* There are certain affect words and certain nonverbal cues of facial expression, body position and movements, and voice qualities associated with these feelings. Your awareness of these cues can assist you in accurately identifying the feeling state of the client and the affective components of his communications.

EXERCISES

To give you practice in identifying nonverbal and verbal affect cues, complete the following exercises:

A. Pick a partner. One of you will be the speaker; the other will be the respondent. After you complete the exercise, reverse roles and repeat the exercise.

　1. The speaker should select a feeling from the following list:

　　contented, happy

　　puzzled and confused

　　angry

　　discouraged

Do not tell the respondent which feeling you have selected. Portray the feeling through nonverbal expressions only. The respondent must accurately identify the behaviors you use to communicate the feeling and should infer the feeling you are portraying. After he has done so, choose another and repeat the process.

[3] G. F. Mahl, "The Lexical and Linguistic Levels in the Expression of Emotions," in P. H. Knapp (ed.), *Expressions of the Emotions in Man,* (New York: International Universities Press, Inc., 1963), p. 84.

2. The speaker should select a feeling from the following list:
surprise
elation or thrill
anxiety or tension
sadness, depression
seriousness or intensity
irritation or anger

Do not inform the respondent which feeling you have selected. Verbally express the feeling in one or two sentences. Be certain to include the word itself. The respondent should accurately identify the feeling in two ways:

a) restate the feeling using the same affect word as the speaker
b) restate the feeling using a different affect word but one that reflects the same feeling

For example:

Speaker: "I feel *good* about being here."
Respondent: a) "You feel *good*?"
              b) "You're *glad* to be here."

Choose another feeling and complete the same process.

B.   Complete the following exercise in verbal affect identification.
   1. Read the following client statements taken from actual interview typescripts.
   2. Identify the affective component(s) in each statement by written sentences and underline the affect word of each client's communication as in the following example:

   Client: "I'm not the type that would like to do research or uh things that don't have any contact directly with people. I *like* to be with people you know—I feel at home and secure with people.

Note: The affect word of *like* is identified.

The following affective components are identified by written sentences using the first person:

1. I enjoy being with people.

2. People help me to feel secure.

3. _____.

If there is more than one affective component within a given client communication, please * (asterisk) the one you feel has the greatest bearing on the client's concern. In the above example, asterisk either 1 or 2, depending on which has the greater bearing in your opinion.

Client statements:

1. "Well, uh, I'm happy just being in with people and having them know me."
2. "And, and uh you know they always say that you know some people don't like to be called by a number, well I don't either."
3. "In speech I'm uh well in speech I'm not doing good because I'm afraid to talk in front of a bunch of people. . . ."
4. "I would love to go back to Germany; I think it's really fabulous."

VERBAL RESPONSES
TO AFFECTIVE CONTENTS:
FUNCTIONS AND TYPES

It is too simplistic to say that the counselor communicates understanding of client feelings through attitudes such as empathy and positive regard. Although empathy and positive regard are necessary to the counseling relationship, the means for communicating these conditions also must be identified. Two primary reasons why the counselor may not respond to client feelings are (a) he doesn't know what would be appropriate ways of responding, and/or (b) the counselor "blocks" upon recognizing the client's feelings.

Blocking refers to the counselor's reaction to client feelings in ways which reduce or restrict his helpfulness. For example, the counselor may accurately identify the client's feelings of anger but avoids responding to these feelings for several reasons. He might be afraid that the client will leave if the interaction gets too intense. He might not trust his own judgment and be afraid that he will turn the client off with an inaccurate response. He might fear that acknowledging the feeling would produce a flood of more intense feelings that he would be incapable of handling. Or, the counselor might have similar feelings that might be aroused. Client feelings related to sex, self-worth, achievement, etc. are also potential blocks.

Knowing how to respond to client feelings with empathy and positive regard takes more than the possession of these attitudes. The counselor must make sure that these attitudes are communicated through his words, statements, and timing. It is possible to identify certain counselor responses that will assist you to discriminate among affective contents, and communicate your understanding of the client's feelings at the same time. Two such responses are:

Reflection of feelings
Summarization of feelings

---

13. Before anything else, the counselor must communicate his understanding of the client's _____.

REFLECTION OF FEELING

The reflection of feeling response is distinctly different from the restatement response, but the two are often confused. As indicated in the previous chapter, the restatement is a paraphrase by the counselor of all or a portion of the *cognitive* content present in a client's response. A client's response might contain both cognitive and affective topics. Whereas the restatement is the paraphrase of the *cognitive* portion, the reflection is a paraphrase of the *affective* portion. The reflection of feeling accomplishes precisely what its name indicates; a mirroring of the feeling or emotion present in the client's message.

The reflection of feeling response can occur at different levels. That is, the counselor can, at the most obvious level, reflect only the surface feeling of the client. At a deeper level the counselor may reflect an implied feeling with greater intensity than that originally expressed by the client. The more obvious level occurs when the counselor reflects an affect message that is *overtly* present in the client's message by using a *different* affect word but one that captures the same feeling and intensity expressed by the client as in the following example.

Client: "I feel really mad that you interrupted me."
Counselor: "You're very angry about being interrupted."

Answer to Item 13 is **feelings.**

---

14. A reflection of feeling is used to reflect the feeling of the client back to him, whether the feeling is directly expressed or only

_____.

The second kind of reflection occurs at a deeper level. This one mirrors an affect message that is only *covertly* expressed or implied in the client's message. Consider, for instance, the implied affect message in the example of: "I think we have a really neat relationship." The feeling inherent in the words refers to a positive affect message of like, enjoy, pleased, and so forth. Thus a reflection that picks up on the implied feeling in this communication might be among the following:

> "Our relationship is important to you."
> "Some good things are in it for you."
> "You're *pleased* with the relationship."

The answer to Item 14 is **implied.**

This reflection that occurs at a deeper level not only mirrors the *covert* feeling but also must at least *match* the *intensity* of the client's feeling and perhaps even reflect *greater* intensity of feeling. Furthermore, the most effective reflection is one that emphasizes what it is the client *anticipates;* in other words, one that acknowledges the *implied admission* of the client's message. Consider this sort of reflection in the following example: note that the counselor reflects back the covertly implied feeling with a greater intensity of affect, and acknowledges the implied admission; that is, what the client would *like* to do or feel.

> Client: "I feel like I have to be so responsible all the time . . ."
> Counselor: "Sometimes you'd feel relieved just to forget all that responsibility—to say 'to hell with it'—and really let go."

Although empathy and understanding of feelings are not in and of themselves a panacea, they do serve some useful functions in the counseling process. For one thing, the presence of empathy enhances emotional proximity, creating an atmosphere of closeness and generating warmth. Secondly, empathy contributes to a sense of self-acceptance. When one person feels really understood by another, there is often a feeling of relief like: "Gee, I'm not so confused and/or mixed up after all," and a sense of acceptance about oneself, such as: "This other person has understood me without condemning the way I think or feel."

When dealing with clients' emotions, beginning counselors often fall into traps. The first trap deals with the counselor's own sense of security in handling the client's feelings. Many counselors, out of their own insecurity in the situation, will do one of the following inappropriate things that do not communicate counselor understanding of feelings:

1. Probe for further information.

Here, rather than to reflect the feelings, the counselor will ask a question as in the following example:

Client: "So I'm wondering if you could help me find a new major— I suppose if I did find one I'd just bungle things again."

Counselor: "What was your old major?"

Although probes are often useful and information is often needed by the counselor, the *first task* should be to *communicate understanding of feelings,* as in the reflection of feeling response which, to the above example was:

"You feel that it's pretty futile to try again."

---

15. Often out of insecurity in handling feelings, the counselor will inappropriately respond to the client with a _____.

Two other common errors made in response to the client's feelings have been identified by Ginott.[4] They are:

1. Responding to the event rather than the feelings involved, as in the following example:

Client: "I really felt left out at that party."

Counselor: "Did you go to the party with someone or by yourself?"

A better response, a reflection of feeling, might be:

"You might have felt alone there."

2. Responding to something general and abstract rather than specific, as in this example:

Client: "I just can't seem to make it here at school with the courses."

Counselor: "They (the courses) can make you work."

It would have been better to respond to the client and not the courses, as in the following example of a reflection of feeling:

---

[4] Hiam Ginott, *Between Parent and Child* (New York: Avon Books, 1965), pp. 30–32.

"You seem to feel pretty discouraged with school and all."

Answer to Item 15 is **question** or **probe**.

---

16. Two common errors made in attempting to respond to client feelings have been identified by Ginott. They are responding

to the event rather than the (a) _____
and responding to something general rather than something

(b) _____.

SUMMARIZATION OF FEELING

Summarization of feeling is very similar to reflection of feeling in that it is a response that discriminates between different affective components of the client's communication and communicates understanding of the client's feelings by the counselor. The basic difference in the two responses is one of *number* and quantity. The reflection of feeling responds to only *one* portion of the client's communication, whereas the summarization of feeling is an integration of several affective components of the client's communication. Thus, summarization of feeling is really an extension of reflection of feeling. "However, in this case, the counselor is attending to a broader class of client response and must have the skill to bring together seemingly diverse elements into a meaningful Gestalt." [5]

Answers to Item 16 are (a) **feelings** and (b) **specific**.

---

17. Summarization of feelings is similar to reflection of feelings.

Summarization of feelings is an integration of (a) _____

_____ affective components of the client's communication

and thus is a bringing together of (b) _____
elements of the client's communication.

---

[5] A. E. Ivey, C. J. Normington, C. D. Miller, W. A. Morrill, and R. F. Haase, "Microcounseling and Attending Behavior: An Approach to Prepracticum Counselor Training," *Journal of Counseling Psychology*, 15 (1968), Part 2, p. 1.

Essentially, like the reflection of feeling, summarization of feeling involves reflecting the feelings of the client in your own words. Again, this involves not just one feeling, but a bringing together of several feelings into a significant pattern. An example of summarization of feelings is the following:

> Client: "The last few months I haven't felt like having any recreation at all . . . I don't know why . . . it just doesn't appeal to me . . . last night I almost had to force myself to go to a dorm party . . . I used to go to all the dances when I first came to college, but now I don't care to."
>
> Counselor: "You feel that even things that you were quite interested in at first now seem less and less interesting . . . you don't know why that is, but it seems that way."

Summarization of feeling is often used instead of reflection of feeling when a client's communication contains many different affective elements, rather than just one or two. It can also be used effectively when the interview appears to be "stuck" or "bogged down."

For example, when one topic has been covered repeatedly or when a dead silence occurs during an interview, summarization can increase the interview pace. By tying together various topics, summarization can identify a central theme. It also provides direction for the interview, and, thus, may furnish the needed initiative to get the interview going again.

Answer to Item 17 is (a) **several** and (b) **different**.

EXERCISES

For the following counselor-client interactions, please observe the following directions:

1. Read each interaction carefully.
2. For each client statement, identify, by writing sentences, the various affective components of the communication.
3. For each client statement write your own response to the affective portion(s). Use both a reflection of feeling and a summarization of feeling for each client statement.
4. For each interaction, analyze the written counselor statement according to whether or not it is an appropriate response to the affective components of the client's communication. Then rate each of the written

counselor responses on a scale from 1 to 5, with 1 being "completely inappropriate" and 5 being "completely appropriate."

5. Discuss the rationale for your ratings with someone else.

Counselor-Client Interactions

Client: "I don't mind school too much, I like it, you know, but I just want to get away and do something different."

Counselor: "School can be boring at times."

(1   2   3   4   5   )

Reflection of feeling: _____

_____

Summarization of feeling: _____

_____

Client: "Actually I'm not looking for any kind of answer. It would scare me half to death if I got one. (Laugh) Then I would wonder what was wrong with me."

Counselor: "There's no need to worry about that."

(1   2   3   4   5   )

Reflection of feeling: _____

_____

Summarization of feeling: _____

_____

EXERCISE

With your triad, complete the following exercise:

1. One of you, designated as the speaker, should share a personal concern with the respondent.
2. The respondent's task is to respond *only* to affective topics using only the two responses covered in the chapter: reflection of feeling and summarization of feeling.

3. The observer will use the Observer Rating Chart (pages 85–86) to keep track of the number and kinds of responses used by the listener. This feedback should then be given to the listener.

4. After interacting in one triad for approximately ten minutes, reverse the roles.

RECOMMENDED READINGS

BRANNIGAN, CHRISTOPHER and HUMPHRIES, DAVID, "I See What You Mean," *New Scientist* (May, 1969), pp. 406–8.

The authors describe facial expressions and body gestures as "more primitive" communication than words, and categorize facial and body positions by the type of message being conveyed.

EKMAN, PAUL and FRIESEN, WALLACE V., "Nonverbal Leakage and Clues to Deception," *Psychiatry,* 32 (1969), 88–105.

The authors have drawn upon their extensive research to describe how our nonverbal behavior often gives away feelings that we think we are concealing.

———, "The Repertoire of Nonverbal Behavior: Categories, Origins, Usage and Coding," *Semiotica,* 1 (1969), 49–98.

Ekman and Friesen present an excellent discussion of what they call "affect displays" and their relationship to behavioral consequences.

MEHRABIAN, ALBERT, "Communication Without Words," *Psychology Today,* (September, 1968), pp. 53–55.

Mehrabian distinguishes between verbal and vocal messages and also discusses facial expression and posture.

OBSERVER RATING CHART

Counselor Response	Type of Counselor Response	
	Reflection of Feeling	Summarization of Feeling
1.		
2.		
3.		
4.		
5.		
6.		
7.		
8.		
9.		
10.		

	Reflection of Feeling	Summarization of Feeling
11.		
12.		
13.		
14.		
15.		
16.		
17.		
18.		
19.		
20.		

9

Discrimination Between Cognitive and Affective Kinds of Client Communications

You have seen in the chapter on *Responding to Client Cognitive and Affective Content* that there are many alternative ways of responding to any client statement. Since your responses greatly influence the nature of topic development, you will be faced with the decision of which kind of content to respond to, and thus, to emphasize. Very often, the client's particular response contains both a cognitive message and an affect or "feeling" message. Typically, in early interviews, the affect message is disguised. The disguise may be thin but nonetheless necessary to the client. It is his way of protecting himself until he can determine to what kinds of things you are willing to listen. Once you are able to hear the affect message (and this comes with practice), you will have to make some decisions. It is important that you respond to that portion of the client's communication that you think is most significantly related to the client's concerns. The process of choosing between client cognitive and affective topics is called *discriminaton*. Whether you choose to respond to the cognitive portion or the affect portion depends largely on what is happening in the interaction at that moment, and on what the client needs. In other words, choosing to respond to the cognitive content serves one objective, whereas choosing to respond to the affect message serves another *objective*.

---

1. Choosing to respond to either the affective or cognitive portion

of the client's communication depends largely on your _____

_____.

Some approaches (for instance, phenomenological) favor almost an exclusive emphasis on affect, whereas others (such as rational-emotive, reality therapy) suggest that the primary emphasis should be on cognitive process. Of course, there are many variables influencing this sort of emphasis. In working with one client who intellectualizes frequently, the counselor may focus primarily on affect in an effort to get the client to recognize and accept his feelings. However, the same counselor, with another client who intellectualizes, may choose to emphasize cognitive elements if the counseling time is too limited for the client to feel comfortable with emotions after his primary defense has been removed. There are certainly times when emphasis on the affective takes precedence over the cognitive area and vice versa. Generally during the interview process, though, it is important to respond to both affective contents and cognitive topics. This is because, for all clients, there are times when feelings govern behavior and times when the behavior and its consequences govern or influence feelings. The important point is not which comes first, but what might be the most effective intervention strategy.

The answer to Item 1 is **objective** or **goal**. If this answer was not obvious to you, it would help to re-read page 87.

---

2. For all clients there are times when feelings _____
behavior and vice versa.

SETTING THE STAGE
FOR AFFECT

In earlier chapters it was noted that, at the outset, it is important to get the client to talk. The client must be able to talk about himself, identify and express feelings, identify his or her own behaviors, and relate to the immediate present or the "here and now." Strong feelings of vulnerability on the client's part may prevent him from doing anything other than responding to his own needs for defending and protecting himself. Reduction of these feelings can release energy previously used by the client for preserving his own image and make that energy available for growth and change. It is *only* at this point that the client can talk about himself and identify and own his feelings and behaviors.

Thus, your initial objective, or first *process goal,* is to reduce the client's initial anxiety. Your first strategy, therefore, with every client is an *exploratory* one; you must determine the effect your behavior has on the client by his initial responses to you.

The correct answer to Item 2 is **govern, influence,** or **cause.** If you had trouble with this, go back to page 88.

---

3. **In the discrimination process the counselor's first strategy with each client is an** _____ **one to determine the effect of counselor response on client behavior.**

Generally, responding to *affect* early in the counseling process is the best strategy for reducing client anxiety. This communicates your acceptance and understanding of these feelings to the client. However, with some clients who avoid emotion and intimacy, your response to their affect message may only induce greater anxiety. With this kind of client you will have to modify the strategy and respond then to cognitive topics: find out how he thinks and what kind of ideas he has.

The correct answer to Item 3 is **exploratory.** See page 100 for further information about this.

---

4. Responding to _____ early in the counseling process is often the best strategy for reducing client anxiety, except with clients who are easily threatened by feelings.

Counselors who always emphasize feelings to the exclusion of behavior, and vice versa, impose certain limitations on the counseling process. Some of the limitations of responding only to feelings include the following:

1. Responding only to feelings is unrealistic and therefore reduces the possibility of the client being able to generalize aspects of the counseling relationship to other relationships. For most clients it is highly unlikely that any of their friends or family would take only their feelings into account.

2. Responding only to feelings fosters an internal focus to the exclusion of the world around the client. The client may become so preoccupied with himself that the level of his other relationships deteriorates even more.

3. Responding to affect induces catharsis; that is, the ventilation of pent-up feelings and concerns. For some clients this may be all that is necessary. For other clients this is not a sufficent goal. With catharsis there is a greater possibility of reinforcing "sick talk"; that is, the counselor's responses to feelings may only generate more client negative self-referent statements.

Answer to Item 4 is **affect**.

5. Responding only to affect reduces the _____ of the counseling relationship to other relationships the client is engaged in outside the counseling office.

Responding primarily to cognitive contents presents the following limitations:

1. It may reinforce the intellectualization process; that is, it may encourage the client to continue to abstract and deny feelings that are actually influencing his behavior.

2. It may not provide the opportunity that the client needs to share and express feelings in a nonjudgmental setting. The counseling relationship may be the only one in which a client can feel that his emotions (and consequently, himself) won't be misunderstood.

Again it must be stressed that the initial strategy in the discimination process is an *exploratory* one. All clients will respond differently to your emphasis on feelings and behaviors. Ways in which you may respond with discrimination to the client, and some general effects of responding to feelings and behaviors may merit closer study.

The correct answer to Item 5 is **generalizability** or **relevance.**

TYPES OF DISCRIMINATIVE RESPONSES
FOR COGNITIVE AND AFFECTIVE CONTENT

There are several counselor responses that are useful as discriminators for either cognitive or affective portions of the client's message. There are responses that can place emphasis upon one component of the message, to the exclusion of other parts of the client's response. Three particularly useful responses are the *accent,* the *ability potential,* and the *confrontation.*

THE ACCENT.   The accent is a one- or two-word restatement that emphasizes a very small portion of the client's communication. Its effect is that of a question or a request for clarification or elaboration. For example, the client may say:

> Client: "I'm having a hard time deciding which college to attend, uh . . . I'm not used to making decisions so it's really perplexing to me."
>
> Counselor: "Perplexing?" (Accents an affect word)

What other words could the counselor have accented in this client response?

1._____ which would emphasize: cognitive   affective

2._____ which would emphasize: cognitive   affective

Model Answers:

1. "Hard time?"
2. "To you?"

Choosing "hard time" would have emphasized the affective portion, but accenting "to you" would have emphasized the cognitive part of the communication.

---

6. The accent is a one- or two-word _____
of the client's preceding response.

The use of the accent places emphasis on a particular thought or feeling. Usually it encourages the client to clarify or expand upon his previous statement, since it suggests to him that the counselor isn't sure he understands the client. It is used most appropriately to highlight a word that seems vague and abstract. Hence, it elicits specificity from the client.

The accent may be used to respond to either the affect or the cognitive message. The client must have used an emotionally-laden word in his message in order for the counselor to accent the affect. This is one limitation of the accent. For example:

Client: "I don't think I will make the grades to stay here."

The counselor has no affect word to accent in this statement. However he could accent the cognitive portion by saying: "Here?" (ACCENT). However, if the client said:

Client: "I'm afraid I won't make the grades to stay here."

Then the counselor could respond with: "Afraid?" (ACCENT). The word *afraid,* which is an affect-type word, can be accented or emphasized, thus inviting the client to elaborate on his emotional reaction to the possibility of not doing well enough to stay in school. Try your skill with the accent in the following client statements:

a) Client: "Things seem pretty bad now."

You: "_____" (emphasizing cognitive or affective?)

b) Client: "I don't know what to do about it."

You: "_____" (emphasizing cognitive or affective?)

See page 94 for the possible responses to this exercise.

The answer to Item 6 is **restatement** or **repetition.**

---

7. If the client's response doesn't contain an emotional word, then the accent can be used to emphasize the _____ message.

THE ABILITY POTENTIAL. The ability potential response is one in which the counselor suggests to the client that he has the ability or potential to engage in a specified form of activity. It can be used either as a response to some cognitive portion or to some feeling expressed in the client's communication. It not only reinforces the client's sense of control and management of his own life and affairs, but also communicates the counselor's faith in the client's ability to act on his own. The ability potential can be used to suggest a course of action that is potentially beneficial to the client.

The answer to Item **7** is **cognitive**.

8. The ability potential response is a statement characterized by the suggestion of a _____ activity or endeavor that the client has the potential for entering or pursuing.

If your client were to say:

"I don't know where I'm going to get the money to pay that bill."

You could say:

"You could work for a semester and earn the money."

In other words, you are suggesting to your client that he has the ability or the potential to pay the bill should he work for a semester and earn the money. Typically the ability potential response begins with "you could," or "you can." Like all of the other types of counselor responses that you have been learning, it can be overused. When that happens, it begins to sound unreal, hollow, and meaningless. It is used effectively as a means of identifying alternatives available to the client. It is *mis-used* when, in over-simplification, the counselor attempts to suggest or prescribe something as a panacea. The effect of this is to negate or hide the client's feelings of concern.

Answers to Accent exercise on page 92:

a. "Things?" (cognitive); "Bad?" (affective); "Now?" (cognitive)

b. "Don't know?" (cognitive); "It?" (cognitive)

Make two ability potential responses in the following client statements:

Client: "I don't know what he'd do; I'm just hanging in thin air because I don't know how he feels about it."

You: "_____

_____."

Client: "I think I'd like to teach but I don't know what the requirements and qualifications are."

You: "_____

_____."

The answer to Item 8 is **future**. The ability potential suggests a **future** activity.

---

9. The ability potential response should identify _____

_____ available to the client.

THE CONFRONTATION.   One of the most useful counselor responses is the confrontation. The word itself has acquired some excess emotional meanings. The confrontation is sometimes misconstrued to mean lecturing, judging, or acting in some punitive manner. A more accurate notion is to regard the confrontation as a response that enables the client to face what he wants or feels he needs to avoid. The avoidance might be a resistance to his own feelings or to another person, including the counselor and counseling relationship. The avoidance is usually expressed as one part of a *discrepancy* present in the client's behavior. Thus the confrontation helps the client to identify a contradiction, a rationalization or excuse, and a misinterpretation.

The answer to Item 9 is **alternatives** or **options.**

---

10. The confrontation response recognizes _____
in the client's messages.

The discrepancy or contradiction is usually one of the following types:

1. A discrepancy between what the client says and how he behaves (i.e., the client who says he is a quiet type, but in the interview, he talks freely).
2. A contradiction between how the client says he feels and how his behavior suggests he is feeling, (i.e., the client who says he is comfortable but continues to fidget).
3. A discrepancy between two verbal messages of the client (i.e., the client who says he wants to change his behavior, but in the next breath places all blame for his behavior on his parents or on others).

The answer to Item 10 is **contradiction, discrepancy,** or **avoidance.**

Operationally, the confrontation is a compound sentence. The statement establishes a "you said – but look" condition. In other words, the first part of the compound sentence is the "you said" portion. It repeats a message of the client. The second part of the compound sentence presents the contradiction or discrepancy, the "but look" of the client message. For example:

> "You say school isn't very satisfying, but your grades are excellent."
> "You keep putting that job off, and eventually you're going to be back in the same trap of being mad at yourself."

The first part, or the "you said" portion, may not be stated by the *counselor*. It may be implied instead, if the client's discrepancy is obvious. For example:

> Client: "I just can't talk to people I don't know."
> Counselor: "(You say etc. [implied part]) But you don't know me."

Using the confrontation suggests doing just what the word implies and *no more*. The confrontation in both the "you said – but look" conditions *describes* client messages, *observes* client behaviors and *presents* evidence. However the confrontation should *not* contain an accusation, evaluation, or problem solution.

The confrontation serves several important purposes:

1. It assists in the client's achievement of congruency; i.e., a state where what he says and how he behaves correspond.
2. Its use establishes the counselor as a role model for direct and open communication. That is to say, if the counselor is not afraid to confront these contradictions, perhaps the client can be less afraid of them.
3. It is an action-oriented stimulus. Unlike the reflection stimulus that mirrors the client's feelings, the confrontation mirrors the client's behavior. It is very useful in initiating action plans and behavior change on the client's part.

Try out the confrontation in these client statements:

Client: "I'd really like to take the course, but the grade contract is really tough."

You: "_____

_____."

Client: "I'm not really angry at my father; he's been doing this to me all my life."

You: "_____

_____."

DISCUSS YOUR RESPONSES WITH SOMEONE.

---

11. The confrontation presents "you said – but look" conditions in which the counselor describes but does not _____.

EXERCISES

Instructions:

A.   In the client statements below, identify the *affective* and *cognitive* components of each; discriminate between the alternatives, then write an appropriate counselor response for each. Limit your responses to accent, ability potential, and confrontation. The type of response to use for each client statement is specified below in parentheses. Tell whether you responded to the affective or cognitive portion. Give your rationale for doing so.

Client 1:   "On weekends I could stay here—I could probably get dates, but I don't stay here. I go home, or I go to my friends, 'cause I hate staying, just staying right here."

Counselor: (accent)

Client 2:   "I don't know how to act when I'm out on a date. I don't know what to do."

Counselor: (ability potential)

Client 3:   "In speech, uh I'm not doing good—the other day uh my instructor he says to me uh you talk like you—like a whisper as if you're trying to get away."

Counselor: (confrontation)

Client 4:   "Most of the time uh well I just like to be alone—but uh well here it is really nice. I like being uh here. It helps me feel better."

Counselor: (accent)

Client 5:   "Well I'm kind of interested in airport management—well the book *Airport* really got to me, but I don't know very much about what that kind of job involves."

Counselor: (ability potential)

Client 6:   "I mean I usually do feel much more comfortable alone—most of the time when I'm with someone else or uh with people, I just feel kind of clammy and nervous you know."

Counselor: (confrontation)

The correct answer to Item 11 is **evaluate** or **accuse**.

B.   With your triad, complete the following exercise:
1. One of you, designated as the speaker, should talk about yourself with the respondent.

OBSERVER RATING CHART

Counselor Response	Type of Counselor Response		
	Accent	Ability Potential	Confrontation
1.			
2.			
3.			
4.			
5.			
6.			
7.			
8.			
9.			
10.			

11.

12.

13.

14.

15.

16.

17.

18.

19.

20.

2. The respondent's task is to:
   a. identify cognitive and affective topics present in the speaker's communication
   b. make a choice as to which topic you'll respond
   c. respond using only the three responses covered in the chapter: accent, ability potential, confrontation
3. The observer will use the Observer Rating Chart (page 98) to keep track of the number and kinds of responses used by the respondent. This feedback should be given to the respondent.
4. After approximately ten minutes of interaction, reverse the roles.

EFFECTS OF RESPONDING
TO AFFECTIVE CONTENTS

The importance of responding to client feelings as an anxiety reduction tool has already been mentioned. Generally speaking, responding to affect diminishes the intensity of feelings. For instance, responding to (accepting) strong feelings of anger expressed by the client will reduce their intensity and assist the client in gaining control of them.

The expression of feelings may be an important goal for some clients. Some people have had so little experience or opportunity to express their feelings openly that to find an acceptant listener provides highly beneficial relief.

Responding to affect with acceptance and understanding can also assist the client to incorporate his feelings and perceptions into his self-image. In other words, the counselor's acceptance of feelings that have been previously denied and labeled as "bad" by the client suggests to the client that he may have mis-labeled his feelings, and thus, himself.

Finally, responding to affect often is the best way to communicate your warmth and involvement with the client. That is, responding to client feelings establishes a high level of trust between you and the client. It is precisely this kind of trust that enables the client to own his feelings, his behaviors, and his commitment to behavior change.

---

12. Responding to affect assists the client in _____ both his feelings and behaviors.

EFFECTS OF RESPONDING
TO COGNITIVE CONTENTS

It has already been noted that responding to cognitive contents can be an anxiety reduction tool for clients easily threatened by feelings. Thus, there are times when rapport with the client is established more quickly by discovering how he thinks before wondering how he feels.

Secondly, it is important to realize that behavior incorporates both feelings and thoughts. In order to effectively solve problems and make decisions, clients have to be able to think as well as to feel. Responding to cognitive contents assists the client in developing and expressing those thought processes involved in problem solving and decision making.

Because behavior is governed by thoughts as well as feelings, clients need to examine not only what they feel, but how they think. Behavior rigidity is often maintained by the kinds of thought patterns present in the client's repertoire. These may need to be discussed and explored before any behavior change can occur.

Although exploration of feelings is useful to most clients, often it is not sufficient for goal achievement. Once the counseling goals have been established, action plans must be developed to produce goal attainment. Responding to cognitive contents goes one step further than responding to affect in that it focuses directly on behavior change.

Once your exploratory objective has been achieved and you have chosen when to emphasize affective content and when to emphasize cognitive content, it is time to develop and implement strategies for each of these areas. There are some strategies which are more effectively used in working with affective material. Other strategies are best implemented when the focus is upon behavior rather than feelings.

The correct answer to Item 12 is **owning** or **accepting**.

10

Selecting the Appropriate Counseling Strategy

Much of what is described as counseling consists of a process or relationship, and the discrimination model implies that the counselor is able to make judgments about his own, as well as the client's, behavior. The counselor makes discriminations that allow him to assess his impact on the client. Furthermore, he must examine and determine throughout the counseling experience that his behavior is meeting the client's goal and not simply reflecting his own theoretical biases.

Once the counselor and client have identified specific client goals, the counselor's expertise comes into play. The skilled counselor must be able to establish rapport and a facilitative relationship, and beyond that, he must possess a repertoire of counseling strategies that can be used to help the client achieve his goals. These strategies become *modi operandi* or plans of action that are designed to achieve specific client outcomes.

The counseling strategies described in this chapter have been used successfully with many clients. They do not exhaust the list of possible strategies, but are selected because they can be used with relative ease by the inexperienced counselor. They have been classified into four categories:

strategies for identifying attitudes and feelings
strategies for changing attitudes and feelings
strategies for identifying inappropriate behavior
and strategies for changing inappropriate behavior.

IDENTIFYING ATTITUDES AND FEELINGS

Often the client is unable to identify or verbalize the feelings and attitudes that are producing his discomfort. When this is the case, the counselor must find ways to help the client examine and express himself before a move toward positive change can occur. The following strategies will give the counselor some options, since a particular strategy may not work for every client or even for every counselor.

Clarification and Reflection
of Client Feelings

Examination and understanding of feelings by the client occurs readily when the counselor clarifies and reflects client feelings as they are expressed in the interview. These include counselor statements such as the following:

Do you mean that?" or "Are you saying that?"
"You seem angry" or "You feel pretty good."

This strategy is most useful when strong feelings prevent the client from taking any action steps toward his goal. Clarification and reflection of client feelings is also helpful when the client seems to be stuck and unable to make progress. That is, a client may be limited to one way of behaving because his response is dictated primarily by his feelings. A wife, for example, may only be able to behave punitively towards her husband who is continually late in coming home until her feelings of resentment have been clarified and expressed. Indeed, most clients who behave in punitive manners (such as, blaming, cajoling, being sarcastic) are unable to respond otherwise until their own underlying feelings of hurt and anger are clarified, reflected, and reduced in intensity.

1. A counseling strategy is a *modus operandi* or a plan of action that is designed to achieve specific _____.

Counselor Expression of Feeling (Modeling)

One of the better ways to help the client to identify and express feelings is for the counselor to *model* this process; that is, the counselor expresses a feeling about himself or about how he might feel if he were the client. The counselor might express his own feelings by saying:

"I think we've really gotten somewhere today and I feel good about that."

The counselor might also express how he would feel if he were in the client's situation by saying:

"If she had treated me that way, I think I would have been pretty angry."

This strategy is particularly helpful to the client who is unable, for whatever reason, to make appropriate emotional responses. For example, a counselor might suspect that one of the contingencies helping to maintain a bright client's poor grades in college is his strong feelings of resentment resulting from parental pressure. However, the counselor can't be sure of this because the client's outward appearance appears docile or neutral. The counselor may attempt to stimulate expression of feelings by modeling how he would feel:

"If my parents put that kind of pressure on me, I'd feel pretty mad. I might not care about doing well."

In using this strategy, the counselor elicits appropriate feelings in the client by demonstrating how another person in the same situation might react.

The correct answer to Item 1 is **objectives** or **goals** or **outcomes**.

2. When the counselor expresses a feeling, he presents a model to the client that _____ appropriate feeling responses.

The Inner Circle Strategy

The "Inner Circle Strategy" developed by Lazarus [1] is another tool useful in eliciting significant feelings from the client. It is particularly helpful with a client who is reluctant to reveal significant material. To introduce the technique, the counselor draws five concentric circles, forming a bull's-eye. The innermost circle is labeled A, the next one B, then C, D, and E. Circle A, the smallest one, is explained to the client as representing his own private territory; the material within circle A being that which the individual shares with no one. The next circle, B, contains data shared only with a few close friends and family. Thoughts and feelings present in the middle circle (C) are typically shared with good friends, whereas the contents of circle D are revelated to general acquaintances. The outer circle (E) represents those basic facts about the person that anyone can discover. The counselor then explains that the material in circle A usually consists of topics in the following areas: sex, anger, dishonesty, financial matters, and personal competence. The point of the inner circle strategy is that the contents of circle A are more or less the same for everyone. Hence the client can feel less reluctant to disclose feelings about these issues knowing that they are shared by most people.

The correct answer to Item 2 is **demonstrates** or **illustrates.**

Confrontation and Encounter

Many clients are aware of their feelings but have difficulty expressing these feelings to others. For some clients expressing positive feelings of warmth and affection is most difficult. Other clients consider the expression of negative feelings of irritation, assertiveness, and anger to involve more risk than any others. The counselor can use the relationship as the starting point for client expression of feelings through the processes of confrontation and encounter. That is to say, when the counselor sees aspects of the client's behavior or feelings of which the client appears to be unaware, he presents this observation for the client's reaction. In these instances the counselor must not only identify the client's feelings, but also encourage their systematic expression as they arise during the interview

[1] Arnold Lazarus, "The Inner Circle Strategy: Identifying Crucial Problems," in John Krumboltz and Carl Thoresen, eds., *Behavioral Counseling: Cases and Techniques* (New York: Holt, Rinehart and Winston, Inc., 1969).

process. Often the client will feel free to confront the counselor with negative feelings before any encounter with positive feelings. In the first instance, the counselor must identify client cues and thereby elicit expression of negative feelings from the client. In the latter instance the counselor may first need to share his own good feelings for the client before the client will feel secure enough to do likewise. Confrontation and encounter processes suggest that the counselor is able to *accept* both positive and negative feelings shared by the client. Thus the client learns that expressing these feelings doesn't automatically have to result in negative consequences.

---

3. The use of confrontation and encounter processes encourages the client to express both positive and negative feelings with-

out incurring _____ consequences.

Searching for Underlying Thoughts

Some clients avoid engaging in desirable behaviors because of the kind of consequences they imagine will result from such action. One useful strategy suggested by Ellis [2] is that of examining the underlying thought processes. Dealing with a client's thoughts about a particular action often reveals that he has certain fears about the outcomes. Usually these are fears such as: "I might be rejected" or "I might make a mistake" or "Someone might not approve of what I did." More often than not his fears are highly irrational, stimulated by a pattern of self-perpetuating, illogical thinking. Once the client identifies what it is about the action he fears, the counselor can challenge the thought processes contributing to the feelings of fear by asking questions such as the two described below:

1. What is the worst thing that could happen as a result of _____?
   After the client identifies the worst thing, then:
2. How would that be so terrible?

The correct answer to Item 3 is **negative** or **unpleasant** or **bad**.

---

[2] Albert Ellis, *How to Prevent Your Child from Becoming a Neurotic Adult* (New York: Crown Publishers, Inc., 1966).

4. Highly irrational thoughts may prevent a client from behaving

appropriately or may _____ **inappropriate**
behavior.

Self-Image Confrontation

A client may not be able to behave differently because of the way he feels about himself. If a client is convinced that he is inadequate, he may start behaving in ways that make him appear inadequate. This becomes a self-fulfilling prophecy. Self-image confrontation is often a constructive way of breaking this cycle. In this strategy the counselor gets the client to confront himself with this distorted view in order to replace it with a more realistic view of self. The counselor may use responses such as the following:

> "You say you're inadequate. What basis do you have for making that statement?"
> "You say you're unattractive, yet girls frequently go out with you. Tell me why they go out with you."

In self-image confrontation, the counselor has the client look at a discrepancy between, or contradiction in, his feelings and behavior about himself. In so doing, the counselor also avoids reinforcing this kind of communication by being supportive or encouraging. Otherwise, a client may learn to engage in self-deprecating statements as a way to obtain praise or support.

The correct answer to Item 4 is **encourage** or **elicit** or **support.**

5. Self-image confrontation is a constructive way of _____

_____ **a negative self-image.**

Dialoguing and Role Reversal

Often a client may report conflicts in his own feelings or thoughts, or in his relationships with other significant people. Often, having a client identify various alternatives and their consequences may reveal a client to be stuck at the point of decision. For example, the client may say,

> "I just don't know what to do. I'd like to go with him but then I also think I should stay here."

Or the client may express hesitation about taking some action because of the possible effects on another person. This may be expressed as:

> "I just can't change majors. I'm afraid it would really bother my folks."

A useful tool in these kinds of conflicts is dialoguing, which involves having the client take the part of *each* person or *each* side of himself. The client is asked to "play out" the conflict through an imaginary dialogue. In the first instance the client is encouraged to talk to both parts of himself. He is told to be the self that wants to go. Then he is instructed to respond as the self who thinks he should stay. The dialogue between the two selves, which occurs in present-tense language, is continued until one part of the conflict outweighs the other.

The correct answer to Item 5 is **challenging** or **combating**.

---

6. Dialoguing or role reversal forces the client to examine both sides of the situation until one side of the conflict appears to

_____ **the other.**

In the example involving a second person, the client is instructed to "put the other person in the chair across from you and imagine he is there." The client begins the dialogue by expressing what he wants and what he resents about the other person. Then he is instructed to change chairs, become the other person and respond to what he just said as himself. He becomes himself again and responds to the other person. Dialoguing in this manner not only serves as practice for the client in expressing his feelings and opinions but also gives a reality base for the probable response from the other party involved in the conflict. This can often remove the barrier that is keeping the client from making the decision and implementing the necessary action steps.

The correct answer to Item 6 is **outweigh.**

CHANGING ATTITUDES AND FEELINGS

All too often, counselors have thought that the expression of feelings led naturally to appropriate changing of feelings. Such an assumption can lead to the reinforcement of the undesired feelings that are producing his difficulties, rather than a change toward desired feelings. The counselor must implement strategies that will help the client change these attitudes and feelings. Among the strategies the counselor may use are:

Successive Approximation of Feelings: Rehearsal and Homework

Many clients desire to make changes in feeling states, making statements such as:

"I wish I could feel happier."

Such changes do not occur overnight. Although the client will not feel completely happy within a short period of time, the counselor can suggest action steps (homework) that will successively approximate the client's desired goal. Together with the client, the counselor might draw up a list of situations the client can enter into which would produce satisfying outcomes. As the client successfully completes such activities, his feeling states will more closely approximate the desired state of happiness. Depending upon the homework specified, the counselor may wish the client to practice or *rehearse* the task during the interview. This permits the counselor to give feedback to the client and make suggestions that will help to insure success outside the interview.

---

7. Successive approximation of feelings requires identification of

_____ **that produce desired feelings, and rehearsal to insure their successful completion.**

Examples of two homework tasks the counselor might suggest to the above client for successive approximations of happiness are described below:

1. Think of a recent instance when you were very happy. Re-create this in your mind. What conditions produced it? Maintained it? Who were you with? What was happening? Spend a few minutes daily this week imagining this situation in your mind.
2. Think of how you'd like to feel as happy. Where would you be? What would you be doing? If you were with some person(s) who would it (they) be? Describe your body cues associated with these pleasant feelings.

The correct answer to Item 7 is **tasks** or **homework**.

Thought Stopping Techniques

Thought stopping techniques are an extension of the illogical thought examination strategy. They are useful when the client's awareness of illogical thoughts has not resulted in any behavior change. Thought stopping goes one step beyond identification and observation of the irrational thoughts. The client is instructed to imagine himself involved in a situation that produces the irrational thought sequence. The client is asked to verbalize the thoughts that are occurring as he imagines the scene. As soon as an illogical thought (one that is self-defeating and based on unrealistic fears and assumptions) is emitted, the thought is sharply interrupted by the counselor who firmly intervenes with the word: "STOP!" Following this command, the client is instructed in ways of changing the thought pattern occurring in his mind. This same process is repeated with the visualization of different situations until the client can easily change the direction of his thoughts on command.

After this technique is demonstrated and practiced within the interview setting, the client is asked to continue using it with reference to the same situation outside the interview on a daily basis. For example, if the client continually ruminates about past mistakes, he will instruct himself to stop when doing so, then change the thought and concentrate instead on a present-oriented situation. After one situation has been mastered, the counselor and client together can use the same procedure to stop other illogical thoughts. The same client, for example, may frequently worry about being wrong. The counselor stops this thought and has the client concentrate instead on thinking about being right. Thus the strategy eliminates self-defeating thoughts by replacing them with constructive, reality-oriented ideas.

---

8. Use of illogical thought examination and thought stopping is

helpful in getting the client to identify _____ consequences preventing him from engaging in desired behaviors.

Role Identification

A counselor may encounter a client who engages in behavior harmful to himself or to others. Additionally, the client may seem unaware of the destructive consequences of his behavior. In working with this kind of client the role identification strategy is useful. This strategy gets the client to identify himself as the target of his own behavior. For example, in working with a client who has been caught damaging cars of other students, the client is instructed to visualize himself as the owner of a damaged car (preferably his own). He is asked to imagine all of the ways he would feel upon finding his car in this shape.

In role identification the counselor is essentially asking the question: "What would it be like if someone did it to you?" Or the counselor may be asking "What would you do in the same or similar situation?" An example of this occurred in a group counseling session. One student presented a problem involving a decision to continue or terminate a relationship with her boyfriend. Immediately the girl was given much advice from the other group members. She was unable to accept the advice and more importantly, unable to identify the alternative courses of action *she* wanted to pursue. Her confusion was reduced when the group leader used the role identification strategy by asking: "If someone else were in the same situation as you, what would you say to that person?"

The correct answer to Item 8 is **feared** or **imagined.**

Related Behavioral Strategies

There are additional strategies that may be used to help the client modify his attitudes or feelings. However, these strategies are more specifically designed to help the client change his behavior and will be discussed in detail in the section entitled "Changing Inappropriate Behavior." The point is that a strong relationship exists between what one thinks about oneself and what one does. Conversely, what one does and the consequences of one's acts has a strong influence on feelings and attitudes about oneself and others. Specific strategies that are relevant to behavior change, but which influence change in attitudes and feelings are: operant reinforcement strategies, vicarious modeling, assertive training, and self-monitoring.

IDENTIFYING INAPPROPRIATE BEHAVIOR

Even after the counselor and client have identified the feelings that are related to the client's problem, what the client can do to remedy his situation may not be obvious. Often the client does not see a relationship between his behavior and the consequences of that behavior. Thus, the child may say that "nobody at school likes me," but may not be able to see that his ways of responding to other children help produce the situation. Or the college freshman may complain that everyone on the hall is continually playing practical jokes on him and making his life miserable. At the same time he may be unable to see that his reactions encourage the others to continue their practical jokes.

To deal with this type of problem, the counselor needs to have strategies available to help the client identify behavior that needs to be changed. Some strategies that have proved helpful are:

Role Visualization

Often a client may describe how he would like to *be,* but cannot identify the kinds of things he would like to be able to *do.* Client awareness in this respect can be fostered by use of the role visualization strategy. The client is instructed to think of someone he knows that he admires and respects—someone who represents his description of how he would like to be. Then the client is asked to list the kinds of things this person is able to do and the kinds of actions this person demonstrates in several different situations. The client is then told to visualize himself as this kind of person. He is instructed to describe what he is like and to specify the behaviors he is engaging in during the visualization process. He is encouraged to try out these behaviors both within and outside the interview setting.

9. Role visualization helps the client translate desires into _____

_____ .

A variation of this is the significant scene re-creation in which the counselor asks the client to re-create three or four memorable past situations related to his problem. The client is told to visualize them and to describe them in the present tense. For example, a client who complains of recently being uncomfortable as the center of attention is asked to re-create and describe several significant scenes in which she felt comfortable as the center of attention. She is instructed to continue this sort of visualization on a daily basis outside the interview.

The significant scene re-creation also is a way to identify the kinds of conditions maintaining the client's behavior. If a client states that "nothing turns him on" the counselor may get an idea of his life style by asking him to relate the three most significant happenings in his life during the previous week.

The correct answer to Item 9 is **behaviors** or **actions**.

Behavior Description and Inventory

One of the best strategies to help the client identify his behaviors is the behavior description and inventory process. This means simply asking the client to describe the kinds of things he does when in a situation. It is important to have the client present specific actions rather than generalized inferences. Behavior description of this sort gives both the client and the counselor an awareness of the kinds of things the client is doing that result in the undesired situation, that is, the contingencies that maintain the behavior. Another way to obtain the same kind of information is to ask the client to inventory a typical day. The client should go through one or more days and briefly list the kinds of things he does and activities in which he engages. Both of these activities will enable the client to see more clearly how his own actions contribute to the undesired outcome(s). Some clients may identify their behaviors but may have difficulty realizing the impact their actions have on other people. With this kind of client a good strategy is the frequency count procedure—simply getting the client to count the number of times he engages in a particular behavior during a given time sequence such as an hour or a day, depending on what is being observed. This process, for example, may help a wife to realize that her husband's complaints about her "nagging" are not entirely unjustified when she finds herself reminding him of five things within one hour.

---

10. **The purpose of the behavior description and inventory is to help the client see how his actions contribute to undesired** _____.

Dialoguing and Role Reversal

Dialoguing and role reversal has been described in the section "Identifying Attitudes and Feelings." This strategy is equally useful for identifying inappropriate behaviors. Often the scene can be acted out between counselor and client in an effort to get at the behaviors that occur between client and other significant people. For example, the client may report that she has been having many arguments with her boyfriend lately and wonders what can be done to prevent the arguments. The counselor might play the role of the boyfriend and ask the client to enact a recent argument. In so doing, the counselor can examine the verbal interactions that occur and can begin to identify which behaviors are related to the disputes.

Video-recording and playback of the role reversal situation is often useful because it permits the client to identify both his appropriate and inappropriate behaviors in a more objective light. If, for example, a client reports difficulty in getting dates, the counselor could video-tape the client role-playing a telephone call to a potential date. Watching the playback might enable the client to assess his behavior in asking for a date. This also gives the counselor an opportunity to discuss and model other more appropriate approach behaviors which the client could then practice and evaluate. If the client has difficulty recognizing and/or accepting some of his inappropriate behaviors, role reversal could be used in which the counselor plays out the client's behavior and the client assumes the part of the girl being asked out.

The correct answer to Item 10 is **outcomes** or **consequences**.

CHANGING INAPPROPRIATE BEHAVIOR

Clients who make commitments to behavior change often are discouraged when they realize that it is impossible to become another kind of person from one counseling session to the next. This kind of disappointment can be alleviated when the counselor encourages the client to take small action steps that result in some progress toward the ultimate goal. Strategies permitting this are:

Successive Approximation of Behavior: Rehearsal and Homework

Disappointment with the speed of behavior change can be alleviated through small action steps that result in some progress toward the goal. Through this process the client's behavior will gradually approximate the level of behavior change desired by the client. It is important that any action step engaged in by the client is successful. Therefore, homework suggested by the counselor should be reasonable in scope. The counselor can observe how the client proceeds as well as make any necessary modifications by having the client rehearse the homework assignment within the interview confines. For example, in working with a client who wants to date but never has, to give initial homework that requires the client to telephone five girls and arrange two dates during the first week would be too overwhelming for that client to even *think* about executing. Instead, a beginning approximation might be having the client imagine telephoning one girl he knows or has met and asking her for a date the following weekend. Since high levels of anxiety generally interfere with performance, having the client role-play the telephone conversation with the counselor can contribute to the overall effectiveness of the plan of action.

---

11. It is important that any action step engaged in by the client be

_____.

In this situation a client's performance may be inhibited because of his own lack of adequate response styles. Having the counselor role-play the client first gives a model for the client. This helps him to identify those behaviors necessary for adequate completion of the homework task.

The correct answer to Item 11 is **successful.**

Behavior Contracts and
Reinforcement Procedures

Clients who are able to identify and own their behaviors often acknowledge that their current actions are resulting in some undesirable consequences. They state how they would like the consequences to be different (goals). They may or may not realize that in order to change the consequences they must first modify the behaviors producing them. Behavior change of any kind can be a slow and painful process requiring much time and effort on the client's part. Therefore, getting the client to make behavior changes is not easy. The counselor must first obtain the client's *commitment* to change. A technique beneficial in gaining the cooperation and commitment of the client is the behavior contract. The contract, which should be written, specifies what actions the client agrees to take in order to reach the desired goal. Furthermore, it contains a description of the conditions surrounding the action steps: *where* the client will undertake such actions; *how* (in what manner) the client will carry out the actions, and *when* (by what time) the tasks will be completed.

Behavior contracts often are more successful when they are accompanied with self-reinforcement. In other words, a client is more likely to commit himself to a contract if he knows there will be some kind of reward resulting from his achievement of the contract terms. The counselor thus encourages the client to provide his own reinforcement. Asking the client to specify what he enjoys doing most in his free time is an effective way of determining an appropriate reinforcer or reward for each individual client. This reward is made contingent upon successful completion of the contract; that is, the client must successfully complete the contract terms before he engages in the activity he chooses as a reward.

---

12. A behavior contract is a strategy used to obtain the client's

_____ **to change.**

Counselor reinforcement also is important in successful implementation of behavior contracts. The counselor can provide reinforcement (anything that serves to increase the frequency of a desired response) easily through verbal approval ("That's great." "I like that.") or by knowledge of progress ("You did very well." "You did the task perfectly." "You've done a great job in improving your study habits."). In order to make the reinforcement most effective it should follow the desired behavior immediately. For this reason a counselor may wish to have the client drop in or telephone as soon as the contract terms are reached. This enables the counselor to provide immediate encouragement to the client. The frequency of the reinforcement is another factor influencing its success. When a client is learning a new behavior, reinforcement is most effective if it is continuous. In other words, the counselor initially would reinforce every demonstration of the client's new behavior. However, after it is incorporated into the client's habits, reinforcement becomes more effective when administered on an interval basis, that is, after every third or fourth demonstration of the behavior. The reinforcement thus becomes occasional rather than continuous. Finally the counselor makes the best use of reinforcement when it is sincerely given and generally felt. To tell a client "I like you" or "You've done a great job" when you don't believe it is a mis-use of this counseling strategy.

The correct answer to Item 12 is **commitment, cooperation,** or **agreement.**

Negative Practice

Often a client may experience such fear about a certain situation that he avoids doing the very thing he needs to do most—practice the difficult responses. Although many other strategies exist for dealing with specified fears and phobias (desensitization; implosion therapy) one of the simplest ones to implement is negative practice. The client is instructed to continually practice or engage in the very behavior that bothers him most. A client who avoids speaking because of possible stuttering is asked to practice stuttering as much as possible. Or a client who is afraid to cry is encouraged to cry continuously for a while. It is important that the client practice to the point of exhaustion. Here, the fear response seems to be reduced partly as a function of the exhaustive use of the fear-producing stimulus and partly as a result of the absurd exaggeration of the fear-producing situation.

Negative practice appears to be effective with specific situational fear such as test anxiety, as well as with more generalized social fears. In using negative practice, the counselor should emphasize to the client that the anxiety response will persist as long as avoidance of the feared situation is maintained. The counselor should then encourage the client to experience the fear deliberately and as fully as possible. Specifically, the client should be told to attend to all bodily sensations accompanying the anxiety responses and to imagine engaging in the actual situation. Continued and persistent efforts are required in order for inhibition of the anxiety response to occur.

---

13. The object of negative practice is to overcome a _____.

Operant Reinforcement Strategies

Operant reinforcement, as presented by B. F. Skinner,[3] states that the likelihood of occurrence of an individual's response is directly related to the consequences of the same or similar responses in the past. More specifically, using an operant-conditioning model in counseling assumes that if the client's behavior is followed by immediate positive reinforcement, the behavior is more likely to occur again in the future. If, however, the behavior is consistently ignored, it is likely to be extinguished; that is, it is likely to be dropped from the client's repertoire. Using an operant-conditioning model in counseling implies that the counselor is systematically reinforcing desired client behaviors (related to the client's goal) while ignoring undesired or inappropriate client behaviors (use of an extinction schedule). Within the interview, for example, a counselor might systematically reinforce (through paraphrase, head nodding, etc.) a client's positive references about himself while ignoring any negative self-referent statements made by the same client.

Often a counselor might have to teach a parent or a teacher the basic principles of operant conditioning to use with problems with their children or in their classes. Usually children who are disruptive are getting some reinforcement for this. Even if the child receives negative attention, it is more rewarding than no attention at all. The child who has continual temper tantrums followed by spanking may interpret the spanking as reinforcement because it is the one time when he has learned he can count on some attention from his father. Similarly, the child who is reprimanded by his teacher for talking aloud in class also may be reinforced by the repri-

[3] B. F. Skinner, *Science and Human Behavior* (New York: The Macmillan Company, 1953).

mand, since this may be the only way he successfully gains individual attention from the teacher.

The correct answer to Item 13 is **fear**.

In each case the counselor must help the teacher or parent to ignore the inappropriate behaviors and start systematically rewarding appropriate ones immediately after they occur. This is easier said than done, primarily because once a child is disruptive, the teacher's set of negative feelings about him increases. The teacher is more likely to consider all of his behavior to be undesirable. Therefore, the counselor must help to sensitize the teacher to the detection of small steps of progress that can be rewarded.

Group Contracting

Often the counselor is faced with not one but many children or students engaged in problem-related behaviors. The teacher who comes to the counselor for advice about her disruptive class is seeking very specific suggestions. This may require the counselor to observe the class behavior and also talk to individual students about the class. Typically, the teacher's behavior is such that it supports the disruptive class behavior. She may find herself reprimanding, cajoling, assigning extra work, assigning detention, or meting out other forms of punishment in an effort to extinguish the undesirable behavior. Skinner [4] observes how frequently institutions attempt to control behavior through punishment, but with only marginal success. Although control through positive reinforcement is more effective and pleasant, it is a rare occurrence. One strategy to use that utilizes positive reinforcement instead of punishment, and is applicable to a large group setting, is that of group contracting. Group contracting is based upon the Premack principle,[5] which says that if you make a less preferred activity contingent upon receiving a reward (a more preferred activity), the least preferred activity is more apt to be accomplished. This can be implemented through the use of group contracting, where both the teacher and students or the counselor and students are involved in setting up the contract. (This is in contrast to a "behavior proclamation" [6] where only the teacher or

[4] B. F. Skinner, *Beyond Freedom and Dignity* (New York: Alfred A. Knopf, 1971).
[5] D. Premack, "Toward Empirical Behavior Laws: I. Positive Reinforcement," *Psychology Review,* 66 (1959), 219–33.
[6] G. L. Sapp, "The Application of a Contingency Management Systems to the Classroom Behavior of Negro Adolescents," (Unpublished paper, University of Tennessee, 1971).

counselor specifies the terms and rewards with no involvement from the learners.)

---

14. Group contracting is based upon positive reinforcement rather

than _____ **.**

Group contracting may be used by teachers, counselors, residence hall assistants, or anyone who works with groups of people. The leader (counselor, teacher, etc.) and the group specify the appropriate and inappropriate behaviors as well as the rewards for engaging in appropriate behaviors. Reinforcement is given to each group member by way of points upon daily completion of any desired behaviors or tasks. Following the accumulation of a certain number of points, the student can engage in an activity selected from a predetermined list of activities.

Vicarious Modeling

In vicarious approaches the counselor helps the client change his behavior by observing the desired behavior of others. The client learns through vicarious experiencing—"as if" the client is actually in the situation himself. The advantage here is that since he is not, this approach can be used with a relatively low amount of threat to the client. The other people whom the client observes are called models in that they demonstrate a behavior that the client wants to imitate. Vicarious modeling approaches can occur in several ways and can be used separately or together for any one client.

The correct answer to Item 14 is **punishment** or **negative reinforcement**.

One vicarious approach, bibliotherapy, involves the presentation of a book or reading material to the client. The book should illustrate characters or examples of situations related to the client's goal. In this way the client learns from drawing upon the experiences of others and their consequences.

Live models can include the counselor who demonstrates the desired behavior of teachers or peers of the client. Although live models have much impact on the client, they are often difficult to use because of the lack of control in insuring their systematic demonstration of the desired behavior.

To correct for this, many counselors make use of symbolic models through audio- or video-tapes or films in which a desired behavior is introduced and presented. All three of these vicarious approaches could be used with a client who wants to improve his study habits. Reading about effective study habits or about successful people and their scholastic efforts is a first step to help the client specify those behaviors involved. Having the counselor or peers demonstrate some effective study habits is another step. Finally the client can listen to an audio-tape or watch a video-tape describing effective study behaviors.

---

15. The object of vicarious modeling is to permit the client to learn

new behaviors by _____ the desired behavior of others.

Observing the following characteristics of vicarious approaches will help insure their success.

1. Modeling seems to have more impact when it is preceded by detailed instructions. In other words, the client should have a good idea of what to look for before observing the model.
2. An effective model must be seen as a warm and nurturing person by the client. In selecting live models the counselor should consider the client's feelings for this person. Other model characteristics such as age, sex, race, and social status should also be examined. The greater the similarity between the client and the model, the more likely the client will be able to identify with the model.

The correct answer to Item 15 is **observing** or **seeing.**

Self-Monitoring

Recent emphases in behavioral approaches suggest the efficacy of any of a number of self-control procedures, of which self-monitoring is the primary one. Self-monitoring involves the client's systematic counting and/or regulating of a given habit, thought or feeling. A counter or a golf score wrist caddy is often used. Self-monitoring seems to interfere with the learned habit by breaking the stimulus-response association and by encouraging performance of the desired response—which is then often reinforced by the individual's sense of progress following its accomplishment.

Self-control procedures, including those to be described in this chapter, are among the best strategies designed to strengthen a client's own investment in the helping process. Self-monitoring procedures eliminate the counselor as a "middle man" and insure greater chances of client success because of the investment made by the client in the strategies for change.

Usually self-monitoring in the form of counting is a way to strengthen a desired response. However, self-punishment can be a self-monitoring procedure that is designed to weaken a particular response. For example, every time the client does not engage in his specified study behavior, he refuses to allow himself to engage in watching his favorite T.V. show; or every time he engages in self-defeating thoughts he snaps his wrist with a heavy rubber band.

Decreasing the frequency of a behavior can also be accomplished through use of a pocket timer. A person can, for example, use such a timer to *decrease* the frequency of cigarette smoking while, at the same time, *increasing* the duration of non-smoking behavior. If a person who has smoked once every fifteen minutes, sets the time for thirty minutes before smoking again, he has increased the duration of non-smoking time and reduced the frequency of smoking as a result.

---

16. Self-monitoring interferes with a learned habit by breaking the

_____ association.

Recent research [7] suggests that self-reward and self-punishment systems may be more effective when used as separate procedures; for example, when both a self-reward and a self-punishment system of monitoring are differentially used to control a client's obsession. Self-monitoring is an excellent way to help a client modify the way he feels, things he thinks, or things he says to himself. A client may, for example, count positive feelings about himself or thoughts of competency. The counting encourages greater frequency of these kinds of thoughts and feelings. A client may count the number of times he tells himself he can do well on a task, or he may count any number of behaviors related to goal achievement: the number of times he tells his spouse "I love you," the number of times he initiates conversations, the number of times he participates in class discussions and so forth.

Counting or quantifying behaviors is the initial step in self-monitoring. Frequency counts of behaviors (or feelings) obtained through use of a

---

[7] F. H. Kanfer and P. H. Duerfeldt, "Comparison of Self-reward and Self-criticism as a Function of Prior External Reinforcement," *Journal of Personality and Social Psychology*, 8 (1968), 201–68.

golf wrist caddy or tally sheet can be recorded at the end of each day by the client. The target behavior may be the number of cigarettes smoked, cigarettes desired, good thoughts about self, or other behaviors that the client may wish to see increased or decreased in frequency. The second, and equally important step in self-monitoring, is charting or plotting the behavior counts over a period of time. This permits the client to see progress which might not otherwise be apparent. It also permits the client to set daily goals that are more attainable than the overall goal.

A good example is the person who wishes to lose weight. By recording his weight twice each day, morning and evening, he is able to plot his progress and set intermediate goals which he can attain. In so doing, he is less likely to become discouraged and more likely to feel rewarded *immediately* when he reaches the end of a "plateau" and begins losing weight again.

The correct answer to Item 16 is **stimulus-response.**

Assertive Training

Assertive training is a strategy designed to help a client strengthen his assertive responses, because a client cannot be assertive and avoiding at the same moment. Assertive training is particularly useful for a client who is submissive, deferent, and has difficulty expressing his own ideas and feelings, particularly when they are in conflict with those in authority around him. Lack of assertiveness may be manifested in some clients by speech pathology (speech errors, pitch breaks, stuttering) and in others by psychosomatic symptoms (headaches, indigestion, nausea, dizziness). In assertive training the counselor begins by having the client identify one situation in which he wants to express his idea or opinion. The client then specifies what behaviors are involved and what he would like to say. The situation is role-played consistently in the interview until the client can be assertive without experiencing any anxiety. Following completion of this task outside the interview, assertive training can continue for other kinds of situations involving self-assertion by the client. The client's successes at assertiveness will soon generalize to other situations as well; that is, it will be increasingly easier for the client to be assertive on his own without the counselor's assistance and rehearsal.

For example, in working with a client who reports difficulty in school achievement, one of the common problems involved is lack of assertive classroom behaviors. The counselor may first need to observe the student in the classroom setting to identify target behaviors. In counting the number of times the student engages in assertive classroom behavior (asking questions, voicing opinions, engaging in group discussion, giving reports, volunteering for blackboard work, initiating conversations with the teacher, etc.), the counselor obtains an accurate idea of the kind of assertive behaviors that are most prevalent in the client's repertoire and the ones the student needs most to strengthen. The counselor can then have the client demonstrate and practice small steps of such assertive classroom behaviors in the interview. When the client is able to demonstrate repeated efforts of a given behavior within the interview, he should be encouraged to practice it on a daily basis in the classroom.

SUMMARY

In working with clients, all of whom present somewhat unique concerns and circumstances, you will find great use for the strategies described in this chapter. However, we would like to make two points of caution.

First, beginning counselors particularly tend to view a strategy as a panacea or cure-all. No one strategy used in isolation from other techniques or used apart from the basic counseling relationship will prove to be that effective.

Second, you must practice using strategies. Like all skills, they will not be as effective when you first start using them, but your skill will grow as you practice.

Finally, keep in mind that counseling is likely to be most effective when a number of these strategies are used in conjunction with each other and when the underlying counselor-client relationship contains a high level of respect and trust.

11

Being in Relationship

Despite the many strategies and techniques utilized in the counseling sessions to achieve client goals and to facilitate the process, the counselor-client relationship is the important underlying component. Ultimately each counselor must ask himself the question: "What can I be in a relationship with another person?" Together, the counselor and client must describe how they relate to one another. This chapter deals with different aspects of a facilitative relationship. It is designed to assist you in expanding your potential for initiating and maintaining the close emotional investment required in the counseling relationship. It will help you in developing your individual capacity for providing some basic conditions of the relationship.

It has been postulated that there are three conditions necessary and sufficient to produce constructive client personality change. Although this statement may be challenged empirically, it can certainly be said that some conditions do facilitate a beneficial relationship and others do not. It also can be said that the client is more likely to reach his goals when a good relationship exists.

Conditions which have been named as important in the establishment of an effective counselor-client relationship include unconditional positive regard, accurate empathy, and genuineness.[1] Although various theorists differ on the outcomes of these conditions, most would agree that if a good relationship is to exist, the counselor must be himself, must value the client, and must be able to understand what and how the client is experiencing.

A constructive counselor-client relationship serves not only to increase the client's chances of attainment of goals, but also serves as a potential model of a good interpersonal relationship—one that the client can use to improve the quality of his other relationships, outside the therapy hour.

You can learn more about this by experiencing and discovering what you can *do* to establish and offer these conditions to the client. Understanding the client's world and life-space has been stressed in previous chapters. Accurate empathy implies just this: that your sense of the client's world fits with his picture of himself. This gives the client the feeling you are "in touch" with him. Empathic understanding involves two primary steps:

1. Accurate sensing of the client's world; being able to see things the way he does;

2. Verbal sharing of your understandings with the client. How do you know when the client feels you have understood? The following client responses involve some sort of recognition on their part concerning the level of your understanding: "Yes, that's it." or "That's exactly right." When your client says something like this following one of your responses, you are assured that he feels you are following and understanding what is occurring within him.

---

1. Empathy involves verbally sharing with the client an accurate

_____ **of his world, his experiences, and his feelings.**

Learning to understand is not an easy process. It involves the capacity to switch from your set of experiences to the experiences of the client, seen through his eyes, not yours. It involves sensing the feelings *he* has, not the feelings you had or might have in the same or similar situation. It involves skillful listening, so that you can hear not only the obvious, but also the subtle shadings of which, perhaps, even the client is not yet aware.

[1] C. Rogers, *Client-Centered Therapy* (Boston: Houghton Mifflin Company, 1951).

The correct answer to Item 1 is **understanding** or **sensing.**

The first step in developing the art of accurate empathy is to acknowledge your good intentions—to indicate that you *want* to understand your client. Can you remember the difference in your own feelings:

1. when someone really seemed to understand what you were saying?
2. when someone completely misunderstood the experience you shared?

Misunderstanding is, of course, inevitable in any relationship, sometimes including the counseling one. Although it is never as helpful as complete understanding, it is still desirable to convey your desire and effort at understanding, as in the following interaction:

Counselor: "If I heard you right you seemed to be really questioning your ability and even your desire to love."

Client: "No that wasn't quite how I meant it."

Counselor: "I would really like to understand this. Could you share a little more about it with me?"

---

2. When misunderstanding occurs in the counseling session, it is still often helpful to communicate to the client your _____ _____ to understand.

Can you recall a relationship where your own strong feelings prevented you from hearing the feelings of the other person? Some counselors' efforts at understanding the client are blocked because their own strong needs to be heard and understood interfere. Developing accurate empathy also means identifying and resolving your own needs so that they do not prevent you from understanding and responding to the feelings and concerns of your client.

The correct answer to Item 2 is **intention** or **desire.**

Understanding *alone* is not sufficient. You also must verbally express to the client your sense of understanding about him. This kind of communication is, in effect, a kind of mirror—a "feeding back" to the client his feelings just as they are for him, without agreeing or disagreeing, reassuring or denying. Accurate empathy involves not only mirroring the client's feelings, but also some parts of the immediate process. For example, if the client continually asks many questions, rather than answering all of the questions and becoming an information-giver, you can, instead, reflect that particular aspect of the process as in the following statement:

"You seem to be asking a lot of questions right now."

or:

"You seem to be wanting a lot of information about this."

or:

"You are asking a lot of questions—I wonder if you are uncertain about what to expect."

Can you think of other aspects of the process that you sometimes might want to mirror? Perhaps some of your ideas included statements such as:

1. "Right now I think what I just said scared you."
2. "It seems difficult to get started today."
3. "You seem reluctant to talk about these feelings."
4. "You seem to be talking about many different topics rather than focusing on one or two."

---

3. Accurate empathy could be compared to a _____ that reflects the client's messages without distortion.

Learning to develop accurate empathy with your client and with other people takes time and practice. It is learning:

1. to hear the client;
2. to let the client know you heard him.

In the space below, list some verbal responses that would reflect empathic understanding to a client.

1. _____

_____.

2. _____

_____.

3. _____

_____.

4. _____

_____.

DISCUSS YOUR RESPONSES WITH SOMEONE.

The correct answer to Item 3 is **mirror** or **image**.

EXERCISES

A.   Using triads, with one person as the speaker, one the respondent, and one the observer, complete the following tasks and then rotate until each person has had an opportunity to react in all three ways.

1. The client should begin by sharing a personal concern with the counselor.
2. The respondent should:
   a. listen to the speaker;
   b. verbalize what he has heard to the speaker.
3. The observer should note the extent to which each of the others accomplished their task and whether any understanding or misunderstanding occurred.

Following a brief (5 minute) interaction, complete (verbally) the following questions:

Speaker: Do you feel the respondent heard what you had to say? Did you feel he understood you? Discuss this with the respondent.

Respondent: Did you let the speaker know you understood or attempted to understand? What blocks within yourself interfered with doing so?

Observer: Discuss what you saw taking place between the speaker and respondent.

Now reverse roles and complete the same process.

B.   This exercise should be completed with a small group of people (minimum: 3; maximum: 10).

1. Each participant is given a piece of paper and pencil.

2. Each participant should complete, in writing, the following sentence:

"My primary concern about being a counselor is _____

_____

_____."

(These should be anonymous.)

3. Papers are folded and placed in the center of the circle.

4. Participants draw a paper. (If one receives his own, all draw again.)

5. Starting with one person, each participant reads aloud the concern listed; then talks several minutes about what it would be like to have this concern. Other participants can then add to this.

This process goes on until each participant has read and discussed a concern. NOTE: When discussing the concern, attempt to reflect only your *understanding* about the world of this person with this concern. Do *not* attempt to give a solution or advice.

6. Following the exercise, members should give each other feedback about the level of empathic understanding that was displayed during the discussion. Sometimes it is helpful to have all group members *rank* each other: who showed the most understanding, who showed the least, etc. Feedback should be specific so participants can use it for behavior change.

RELATING TO THE CLIENT

Often mirroring the client's feelings or parts of the process will involve some discussion about how you and the client relate. Whereas accurate empathy refers to your expression of the *client's* feelings, genuineness and unconditional positive regard deal more with the sharing of *your* feelings. A diagram of this might look like:

ACCURATE EMPATHY   *GENUINENESS, POSITIVE REGARD*
Expression of Client's Feelings   Expression of Counselor's Feelings

Effective counselor-client relationships incorporate *both* aspects of this diagram. Many counselors fall into the trap of "playing the counselor's role" by merely reflecting the client's feelings. Limiting your expression to this presents several problems:

1. It creates insecurity; the client is kept in a constantly ambiguous state about how you feel.
2. There is no role model effect for the client. If you can effectively express *your* immediate feelings, it encourages the client to do likewise.
3. There is no source of feedback other than the client's perceptions. Expression of your feelings gives the client an idea of how he is perceived by others.

Expression of your feelings should not take precedence over understanding the client's feelings. The counseling relationship does not have all the mutuality present in many relationships, such as friend to friend, husband to wife and so forth. Sharing of your feelings is most beneficial when it serves one of the three purposes mentioned above.

---

4. The facilitative relationship involves your expression of your own feelings as well as the _____ feelings.

Before you can express your feelings, you must become aware of them. Ask yourself, for instance, what does it mean to be genuine? Can you tell when you are being yourself or when you are presenting an image that is different from the way you actually feel? In order to communicate genuineness to the client you must first learn to get in touch with yourself and your feelings—to become aware of who you are as an individual and what kinds of thoughts and feelings you have. This involves learning to discriminate between your various feelings and allowing them to come into your awareness without denial or distortion; it means, for example, that when you are happy you can acknowledge that you are happy, or when you are angry you can be aware of your anger.

To assist you in becoming aware of your own thoughts and feelings, pick a partner and spend a few minutes with each other in the exercise of "Dyadic Encounter," that appears below.[2] All you need to do is respond to the open-ended questions as honestly and directly as possible. Both of you should respond to one question at a time.

The correct answer to Item 4 is **client's** or **counselee's.**

---

[2] J. W. Pfeiffer and J. E. Jones, "Dyadic Encounter," *A Handbook of Structured Experiences for Human Relations Training,* Vol. 1 (Iowa City, Iowa: University Associates Press, 1969), pp. 97–107.

DYADIC ENCOUNTER EXERCISE

This dyadic encounter experience is designed to facilitate getting to know another person on a fairly close level. The discussion items are open-ended statements and can be completed at whatever level of self-disclosure one wishes.

My name is . . .
The reason I'm here is . . .

One of the most important skills in getting to know another person is listening. In order to get a check on your ability to understand what your partner is communicating, the two of you should go through the following steps one at a time.

Decide which one of you is to speak first in this unit.

The first speaker is to complete the following item in two or three sentences:

When I think about the future, I see myself . . .

The second speaker repeats in his own words what the first speaker has just said. The first speaker must be satisfied that he has been heard accurately.

The second speaker then completes the item himself in two or three sentences.

The first speaker paraphrases what the second speaker just said, to the satisfaction of the second speaker.

Share what you may have learned about yourself as a listener with your partner. (To check your listening accuracy, the two of you may find yourselves later saying to each other: "Do you mean that. . . ?" or "You're saying that. . . .")

When I am in a new group, I . . .
When I am feeling anxious in a new situation, I usually . . .
(Listening check:) "You're saying that . . ."
The thing that turns me on most is . . .
Right now I'm feeling . . .
(Look your partner in the eye while you respond to this item.)
When I am rejected, I usually . . .
The thing that turns me off the most is . . .
Toward you right now, I feel . . .
When I am alone, I usually . . .

(Listening check:) "Do you mean that . . . ?"

I am rebellious when . . .

(Checkup:) Have a two or three minute discussion about this experience so far. Keep eye contact as much as you can, and try to cover the following points:

How well are you listening?

How open and honest have you been?

How eager are you to continue this interchange?

Do you feel that you are getting to know each other?

Then continue:

I love . . .

I feel jealous about . . .

Right now I'm feeling . . .

I am afraid of . . .

The thing I like best about you is . . .

You are . . .

Right now I am responding most to . . .

---

5. A first step in discovering what it means to be genuine is to learn to be aware of and express your own _____.

Expression of your thoughts, ideas, and feelings follows after your awareness of them. This process might also be called self-expression or *self-disclosure*. Self-expression and disclosure are important ways of letting the client know that you are a person and not just a role; however, self-disclosure should be used appropriately and not indiscriminately in the counseling sessions.

The correct answer to Item 5 is **feelings** or **attitudes**.

---

6. Self-disclosure can be an important component of genuineness in the counseling interview as long as it is used carefully and _____.

It is important not to interpret self-disclosure to mean that the counselor ought to talk about himself, since the primary focus of the interview is on the client. Thus genuineness does not mean that the counselor reveals his own experiences, ideas, and values. It does mean, however, that occasionally it is appropriate and helpful for the counselor to reveal or disclose a particular feeling he may have about the counseling session or about the client. The clue to appropriateness is often determined by the question: "Whose needs am I meeting when I disclose this idea or feeling: the client's or mine?" Clearly the former is the much more appropriate instance of the two.

There are several different kinds of self-disclosure. These include:

1. the counselor's own problems
2. facts about the counselor's role
3. the counselor's reactions to the client (feedback)
4. the counselor's reactions to the counselor-client relationship.

The correct answer to Item 6 is **appropriately** or **with discrimination**.

Usually disclosure in the latter two areas is more productive than any disclosure by the counselor pertaining only to himself. Many times counselors are tempted to share their own problems and concerns when encountering a client with similar problems. In a few instances the counselor may do so to reassure the client his concern is not so catastrophic. But in most other instances a role reversal occurs—the counselor is gaining in sharing this with the client. Recent research indicates that the counselor who discloses at a high level may be perceived as having significantly poorer mental health by the client.[3] Thus, self-disclosure about the counselor's own problems may limit the client's confidence in the counselor as an effective helper.

Similarly, some counselors are tempted to give their life history to the client. Often clients may ask questions concerning information about the counselor. "Are you married?", "What kind of job do you have?", "Are you in school?" are some common types of questions clients ask in seeking facts about the counselor. Often it is best in this case just to give a direct, brief answer and then return the interview focus to the client. If, however, this is a common occurrence with the same client there are

---

[3] R. G. Weigel, N. Dinges, R. Dyer, and A. A. Straumfjorn, "Perceived Self-Disclosure, Mental Health, and Who is Liked in Group Treatment," *Journal of Counseling Psychology*, 19 (1972), 47–52.

other ways of responding. Continual client questioning of this sort often indicates that the client is anxious, feels like he's "on the hot seat" and is attempting to get off it by turning the focus onto the counselor. There are better ways to handle this than by spending the interview disclosing facts about yourself! Alternative ways of responding include:

1. reflecting upon the client's feelings of anxiety:
    "You seem anxious about talking about you now."
2. reflecting upon the process:
    "You seem to be asking a lot of questions now."
3. making a statement about what you see happening:
    "I think you feel like you've been on the 'hot seat' and asking me questions is a good way for you to get off it."

---

7. **Self-disclosure and genuineness does not mean that the focus of the interview is on the _____ experiences and concerns.**

Think about yourself in the following instances.

1. You have a client who describes herself as "shy and retiring." During the third interview she says: "I'd like to be like you—you seem so outgoing and comfortable with people. Why don't you just tell me how you got that way." Do you consider it appropriate to then share some of your experiences with her?
2. You have had one particular client for about seven individual sessions. After the first session, the client has been at least several minutes late for each session and waits until almost the end of the interview to bring up something important to discuss. You feel that the client is infringing upon your time. This is preventing you from giving your full attention and understanding to the client. You have acknowledged to yourself that this is bothering you. Is it appropriate then to go ahead and express this to your client?

The correct answer to Item **7** is **counselor's** or **helper's.**

---

8. **Take a few minutes to think about yourself as the counselor in the two preceding examples. Now write in the space on the next page what you would do in each example for "facilitative genuineness."**

In a very real sense there are no "correct" answers to these two examples in that each counseling interaction is somewhat different. Ultimately, you as the counselor will have to make a decision like this for yourself in each and every instance. Based on the preceding written material, perhaps you did indicate that it would be more appropriate to express your irritation in the second example than to disclose about your experiences in the first. In the first instance there are more productive ways of helping the client reach her goals than sharing facts about yourself. For instance, she would be more involved if you suggested role reversal. You become the client; have her be the "outgoing and comfortable" counselor she sees. In the second instance the client is not fulfilling his share of the responsibility by being late; or he is indirectly communicating resistance that needs to be shared and discussed.

Some counselors are able to acknowledge their feelings and to determine *when* these can best be expressed in the interview, but are not sure *how* to express these kinds of thoughts and feelings to the client. Self-disclosure or expressions of genuineness are often characterized by sharing-and feedback-type statements [4]—statements that convey to the client your sense of what is going on and your feeling about it. These kinds of statements can be illustrated by the following examples:

"I am glad you shared that with me."
"If that happened to me, I think I'd feel pretty angry."
"I don't feel like we're getting anywhere right now."

---

9. Statements such as "I see you doing this and here's how I feel about it" and "I see this going on and it makes me feel this

way" are referred to as (a) _____ and (b) _____

_____ statements.

Sharing and feedback communicate to the client that you have heard or seen something going on, and that you have certain thoughts or feelings about it and want to communicate these. Sometimes you will want to comment not only on what you feel about a specific instance or experience but also how you feel about the client. This will be more effective if your feelings are expressed as immediate ones, that is, expressed in the *present* rather than the past or future. This is the meaning of keeping the process of relationship in the "here and now," using what is going on from moment to moment in each session to build the relationship. It is represented by the type of statement that communicates, "Right now I'm feeling. . . ." or "Right now we are. . . ."

To experience this "here and now" kind of communication, try to get in touch with yourself this instant. What are you feeling this very moment as you are reading and thinking about this page, this paragraph, this sentence? Write in the space below four or five adjectives that express your present feelings. Tune into your nonverbal cues as well (body position, rate of breathing, tension spots, etc.).

---

[4] W. H. Higgins, A. E. Ivey, and M. R. Uhlemann, "Media Therapy: A Programmed Approach to Teaching Behavioral Skills," *Journal of Counseling Psychology,* 17 (1970), 20–25.

The correct answers to Item 9 are (a) **sharing** and (b) **feedback.**

Other examples of sharing kinds of responses are:

Client: "It's hard for me to say so but I really do get a lot out of these sessions."

Counselor: "That makes me feel good to hear you say that."

or

"I'm glad to know you feel that way."

Note that in the counselor's sharing statements the communication is *direct*—it focuses on the counselor's feeling and on the client. It is specific and not generalized as in the following comment:

"I hope most clients would feel the same way."

Such statements should avoid the trap of "counselor language." To always begin a sharing and/or feedback statement with "I hear you saying" or "It seems that you feel" or "I feel that you feel" gets wordy, repetitive, and even phoney. Say exactly what you mean.

---

10. Feelings expressed by the counselor in sharing statements are immediate when expressed in the _____.

Now, with a partner, engage in some sharing type statements that are direct, specific, and immediate. Can you tune into your feelings as you engage in this kind of communication? What does it do for you and what effect does it have on the other person? Jot down some of these reactions in the space provided below. List the sharing statements you have made to your partner.

When sharing statements reflect the expression of the counselor's thoughts and feelings, feedback statements incorporate a description of *client behavior* as well. Some examples of feedback type statements are: Counselor: "When you are continually late to the sessions (client behavior) I feel it is a loss to both of us" (counselor feeling); or, "When you talk about school your face really lights up," (client behavior) and "It makes me feel good to see you so happy about that" (counselor reaction).

You probably are aware as you read, that these examples have several characteristics fundamental to effective feedback processes. Such statements express a feeling acknowledged and *owned* by the counselor, as in "when something happens, I feel thus and so," or "when I see you _____ _____, I think_____." They avoid judgment and evaluation. Most of all they do not accuse or blame as in the following statement: "You are a real problem to work with because you are always late." In other words, they preserve the dignity and self-respect of the other person involved in the relationship. Furthermore, an effective feedback statement does not contain advice; it is not a "parenting" or scolding statement. It also should concern a behavior or attitude the other person has the capacity to change or modify. It would not be helpful for instance, to use the following kind of feedback statement:

"I just don't like the way you look. Why don't you go do something about your complexion?"

Feedback is usually more effective when solicited. Thus, feedback statements that relate to the client's goals or to aspects of the counseling relationship may be better received by the client because of his involvement in this. In any case, though, you can determine the effects of your feedback by the client's reaction. If he is defensive, gives detailed explanation or justification, or makes strong denials, this is a clue that your feedback was not solicited and that perhaps you have touched on an issue too soon. At this point the client needs an indication of your support and acceptance. It is also helpful to mirror the process that you see occurring as in the following statement:

"When I expressed my reactions about our not getting anywhere today, I felt you didn't want to hear that."

Now with a partner, try some feedback type statements that meet the characteristics described in the preceding section. Be sure your responses include a description of your partner's behavior as well as your reactions to it. For example, you might say something like:

"I appreciate (your feeling) your taking the time to talk with me (his behavior)."

List the feedback statements you make to him or to her. What are the effects on you? on the other person? on the relationship?

In some ways, the expression of unconditional positive regard is similar to the experience of facilitative genuineness. Positive regard is often misconstrued as agreement or disagreement with the client. It is an attitude of valuing the client rather than a measure of your level of agreement. To show positive regard is to express appreciation of the client as a unique and worthwhile person.

---

11. The expression of positive regard, a sense of real _____

_____ for the client, can have powerful effects in enhancing the counselor-client relationship.

Think for a few moments about several of your existing relationships. Choose several that you would describe as good interpersonal relationships. Also think about a few poor ones. Can you determine any missing elements in the latter relationships? Chances are your feelings about the other person in the good relationships are more positive. Liking another person has almost a circular effect. For instance, when you value a client, your sense of liking will be communicated to him; this alone will enhance his feelings for himself and add to his appreciation of himself as a worthwhile human being. Counselors typically discover that a better relationship exists with those clients they describe in positive terms. Think now of one of your clients (or a friend) with whom you have some difficulty relating. How do you describe this person? Is it primarily a positive or negative description? If you said "negative" you are focusing on the individual's *limitations*. Sometimes this has to be expressed to the client (or friend) in order to permit feelings of positive regard to develop. Think again of the same person. This time identify two or three strengths of the person. Sometimes thinking of a client in this way can increase your sense of positive regard.

Think of expressing this to the client: (a) those limitations that may be blocking your sense of liking for the client and (b) those strengths that increase your appreciation for the client. The following steps may assist you in expressing this:

1. Picture the other person in your mind. Begin a dialogue in which you express what it is that is interfering with your sense of positive regard. Now reverse the roles. Become the other person. What does he say in response? Then what do you say?

2. Complete the above process again. This time express the strengths you see in the other person; what you appreciate about him. Again reverse the roles. Become the other person. What does he say in response? Then what do you say?

This exercise can be used with any client for whom you have difficulty experiencing positive regard.

The correct answer to Item 11 is **appreciation** or **valuing.**

12. Take a few minutes to think of a person with whom you are currently in relationship and for whom you experience "positive regard." What kinds of things do you do to express your feelings of positive regard for this person? Jot them down.

There is no set answer to the above Item 12 because each person has a little different style of communicating good feelings for another person. The first step is positive regard, though—to feel comfortable enough to express warm feelings to someone else. Being free enough to spontaneously share feelings of regard for another human being is a process that can be learned.

13. Think again for a moment about several of your existing relationships with a few people close to you—perhaps your spouse, parent, child, neighbor, or friend. Then respond, in

writing, to the following questions: What is your level of expression of positive regard to these people? How often do you say things like: I like you; It's nice to be with you; You're good for me; I enjoy you; and so forth?

What is your feeling when you do? What is the effect on the other person? If your expression of these kinds of statements is infrequent, what might be holding you back?

Either now, or later, seek out someone you like and try to express these kinds of feelings to the other person. Then think again about the above questions. Share your reactions with your partner.

In doing this you probably have noted that warmth and positive regard are expressed both nonverbally and verbally. Nonverbally, you show this by facial expression, smiling, and eye contact. You might in fact think of your entire nonverbal stance as communicating a sense of enthusiasm for the other person. In counseling, positive regard is sometimes seen when the physical posture of the counselor mirrors that of the client. Verbally, you express your feelings for another person by statements that reflect a sense of caring and affection, best described, perhaps, by the word *nurturance*.

14. Verbal expressions of positive regard may be described as af-

fectional _____.

Affectional nurturing statements can have a strong effect on the client and on the relationship. They are most effective when used *selectively* and *sincerely*. You probably know the feeling you have about someone who *always* is saying nice things—these statements lose their effect when used constantly.

The correct answer to Item 14 is **nurturance** or **caring.**

Some examples of affectional nurturing statements are as follows:

Client: "I know I shouldn't do that because at those times I'm selfish, yet it's hard for me to always do everything for her first, but I am selfish and that's an even worse way for me to be."

Counselor: "I like you even when you're selfish."

Client: (crying) "I'm sorry I'm crying. They (parents) tell me I am a baby for doing it, but I am so worried, but uh, I'll try not to do it."

Counselor: "It's all right for you to cry with me."

Try to think of some affectional nurturing statements on your own. List them below.

1. _____

_____ .

2. _____

_____ .

3. _____

_____ .

4. _____

_____ .

DISCUSS YOUR RESPONSES WITH SOMEONE.

It has been observed that the counseling relationship should contain the best elements of any effective interpersonal relationship. A facilitative counseling relationship serves as a model that the client can use to improve the quality of relationships outside the counseling room.

The counselor must initiate those qualities that generate and maintain the relationship process. Although the behaviors presented in this chapter can be learned and incorporated into your style and repertoire, "that's not all there is." The integral human element of the counseling relationship cannot exist by the counselor's mechanical manipulation of certain behaviors at given points. The relationship with each client contains its own uniqueness and spontaneity that cannot be systematically controlled prior to its occurrence without the loss of both sincerity and humanness. And, after all, isn't that what people are all about!

RECOMMENDED READINGS

BRAMMER, LAWRENCE, and SHOSTRUM, EVERETT, *Therapeutic Psychology: Fundamentals of Actualization Counseling and Psychotherapy.* Englewood Cliffs, New Jersey: Prentice-Hall, Inc., 1968 (2nd edition).

This book gives one of the most comprehensive treatments of the counseling relationship that exists among current counseling texts. The authors describe strategies for use with special relationship problems, particularly resistance, transference and counter-transference.

PIETROFESA, JOHN, LEONARD, GEORGE and VAN HOOSE, WILLIAM, *The Authentic Counselor.* Chicago: Rand McNally and Co., 1971.

This book concerns itself with those therapeutic conditions essential for producing an effective counseling relationship. It presents a humanistic viewpoint of the counseling process. Self-disclosure and humanness are considered to be two primary qualities of the authentic counselor.

ROGERS, CARL. *Client-centered Therapy.* Boston: Houghton Mifflin Company, 1951.

Rogers discusses and illustrates the use of counselor-offered conditions of accurate empathy, genuineness, and unconditional positive regard. He elaborates on the uses of these attitudes not only to create the therapeutic relationship, but also to promote "constructive personality change" in the client.

12

Implementation of Counseling Skills

Much material has been covered in the previous chapters. As you see your first clients, you may conclude that it is impossible to remember and apply all that you have learned. Some beginning counselors report that their efforts to counsel, using a skills approach, actually hindered them at first. If this is your experience, it will help to know that it is natural, even predictable to feel the pressure to use your newly developed skills and forget the person sitting across from you in the process.

How can this situation be avoided? Perhaps the best approach is to focus your attention *totally* upon the client. Using your client as your focal point will achieve two objectives. First, you will be placing your commitment precisely where it should be. The client must be able to feel that you are working in his behalf. Secondly, by focusing upon the client, you are more likely to implement the skills you have learned. This may sound strange, but it does work in practice. The phenomenon is similar to the person who tries to think out and analyze how he walks. The harder he thinks about the procedure, the more awkward his walk becomes.

The initial anxieties of meeting a "real" client for the first time are debilitating for many beginning counselors. This is a temporary effect, however. As you see more clients, you will think less about some of the fears with which you began. This reduction of fear will permit you to return to the real business of counseling. You will need to assess your style and its effect upon your clients. If possible, you should have someone supervise your sessions from behind a one-way mirror. In case this isn't possible, then you might tape-record your interviews and listen to the tape 12 to 24 hours after the session. You will be amazed at the amount of material you missed during the session, but which is abundantly clear in the re-run. But self-evaluation is more than listening to a re-run of the session. It is at this point that you can afford to be critical of your application of counseling skills. Toward this end, two approaches to evaluation will be described. The first, self-evaluation, is intended to be used when there is no other person available to help you assess your skills. It is a more global evaluation but will help you to examine your personal input into the session.

SELF-EVALUATION

The Counselor Self-rating Form will help you in your assessment of the conditions operating within you as you counsel.[1] It is divided into three parts: Fear of Failure, Fear of Losing Control, and Need for Structure. You will notice that the items under each division are to be scored on a scale from 1 to 10. Record your self-evaluations of the items for the first client you see in the column, labeled "First Client." After completing this first rating, set the form aside. Upon seeing your fifth client, re-rate the items in the column labeled "Fifth Client." At this point you will be able to identify areas that need further attention from you. Where you find a particular item that you know to be a trouble spot, identify a goal for yourself to help you alleviate this problem. Secondly, list the action steps that will permit you to achieve the goal. For example, if you find that you are continuing to worry about the client's getting upset (Item 3, Fear of Failure), you might identify as your goal:

GOAL: To permit the client to cry (or get angry, etc.) without feeling that it is my fault.

ACTION STEPS:
      1. To identify the client's emotional response and relate it to his other responses in the interview.
      2. To identify the relationship between the client's emotional response and conditions in his world that would produce such a response.

[1] Self-rating Form is adapted from a classroom group leader self-rating form originally developed by William A. Poppen, The University of Tennessee.

COUNSELOR SELF-RATING

Rate yourself from 1 to 10 on each item.

1 = not like you
10 = much like you

I. Fear of Failure:

1st Client   *5th Client*

————   ———— Often I ask a question instead of responding to my perceptions of the client.

————   ———— As soon as the client expresses a negative feeling I change the subject.

————   ———— When the client gets upset I want to smooth things over.

————   ———— It is difficult for me to confront the client.

————   ———— The tape recorder bothers me.

————   ———— I worry about being observed by my supervisor.

————   ———— I would hate to do the wrong thing.

————   ———— I can't imagine myself being a successful counselor.

GOAL:

ACTION STEPS:

II. Fear of Losing Control

1st Client   *5th Client*

————   ———— I talk for more than half of the interview.

————   ———— I anticipate what the client might say and say it for him or her.

————   ———— I'm bothered a lot by the thought that interviews are not very helpful.

_____   _____   There are certain topics I feel uneasy about letting the client discuss.

_____   _____   I usually introduce a topic for the client at the beginning of an interview.

_____   _____   Continuity is very important to me; I try to keep the client on similar topics from one interview to the next.

GOAL:

ACTION STEPS:

III.   Need for Structure

1st Client   *5th Client*

_____   _____   I can hardly stand it when I don't understand what the client says.

_____   _____   It irritates me when the client rambles.

_____   _____   I don't know what to do when the client doesn't identify a problem.

_____   _____   I find myself giving new clients many details concerning the interview, taping, etc.

_____   _____   I am unsure about when to deal with feelings and when to focus on behaviors.

_____   _____   I often feel I have to initiate topics to keep the interview going.

_____   _____   I'm bothered by the thought that counseling with some clients seems to have no purpose.

_____   _____   Specific behavioral goals bother me.

GOAL:

ACTION STEPS:

SUPERVISOR EVALUATION

Most counselor trainees view the opportunity for supervision as a mixed blessing. They know that their performance has "blind spots" that are more easily identified by an observer. On the other hand, they feel vulnerable with the prospect of having someone view and assess their interview behavior, particularly when they cannot see that person. There are no easy solutions to this problem. Learning to feel comfortable with your supervisor is uniquely a function of your own goals and the supervisor's awareness of your discomfort. Therefore, you must identify the implications of your counseling goals in terms of your own risk-taking, and you must be prepared to communicate your fears to your supervisor.

The Counseling Strategies Checklist is suggested as one means of assessing your performance. It is divided into categories that conform to the several skills chapters in this text. The supervisor may want to use parts of the Checklist for each interview, rather than attempting to complete the total checklist each time you are observed. The Checklist provides a point of departure for you and your supervisor to discuss the progress of the interview, and your input and its effect upon your client.

One further point might be made in reference to the use of the supervisor evaluation. In Chapter 8 it was mentioned that the counselor often encounters "blocks" as he attempts to respond to his client. He may be able to identify quite accurately the feeling the client is describing, but may not be able to respond to that feeling. This would probably be described by the Freudians as counter-transference. When the client talks about a problem that is also a problem for the counselor, he may feel unqualified to respond, or he may be overwhelmed by his own feelings and unable to respond. It is at this point that a supervisor can be most helpful in counseling the counselor, helping him to work through his own feelings, and identifying ways in which he can manage his feelings the next time the situation arises. To receive this assistance from your supervisor, you must acknowledge to him your own blockage.

Using the Counseling Strategies Checklist

Each item in the CSC is scored by circling the most appropriate response, either Yes, No, or N/A (not applicable). The items are worded such that desirable responses are *Yes* or *N/A; No* is an undesirable response.

After the supervisor has observed and rated the interview, the two of you should sit down and review the ratings. Where noticeable deficiencies exist, you and the supervisor should identify a goal or goals that will remedy the problem. Beyond this, you should list two or three Action Steps that permit you to achieve the goal. After three or four more interviews, have the supervisor evaluate you again, and compare the two sets of ratings to determine whether or not progress was evident.

COUNSELING STRATEGIES CHECKLIST

Part I: Counselor Reinforcing Behavior (Nonverbal)

1. The counselor maintained eye contact with the client.
   Yes   No   N/A
2. The counselor displayed several different facial expressions during the interview.
   Yes   No   N/A
3. The counselor's facial expressions reflected the mood of the client.
   Yes   No   N/A
4. The counselor often responded to the client with facial animation and alertness.
   Yes   No   N/A
5. The counselor displayed intermittent head movements (up-down, side-to-side).
   Yes   No   N/A
6. The counselor refrained from head-nodding when the client did not pursue goal-directed topics.
   Yes   No   N/A
7. The counselor demonstrated a relaxed body position.
   Yes   No   N/A
8. The counselor leaned forward as a means of encouraging the client to engage in some goal-directed behavior.
   Yes   No   N/A
9. The counselor demonstrated some variation in voice pitch when talking.
   Yes   No   N/A
10. The counselor's voice was easily heard by the client.
    Yes   No   N/A
11. The counselor used intermittent one-word vocalizations ("mm-hmm") to reinforce the client's demonstration of goal-directed topics or behaviors.
    Yes   No   N/A

Counselor Reinforcing Behavior (Verbal)

12. The counselor usually spoke slowly enough so that each word was easily understood.
    Yes   No   N/A
13. A majority (60% or more) of the counselor's responses could be categorized as complete sentences rather than monosyllabic phrases.
    Yes   No   N/A

14. The counselor's verbal statements were concise and to the point.

Yes   No   N/A

15. The counselor refrained from repetition in his verbal statements.

Yes   No   N/A

16. The counselor made verbal comments that pursued the topic introduced by the client.

Yes   No   N/A

17. The subject of the counselor's verbal statements usually referred to the client, either by name or the second person pronoun, "you."

Yes   No   N/A

18. A clear and sensible progression of topics was evident in the counselor's verbal behavior; the counselor avoided rambling.

Yes   No   N/A

PART II: *Opening the Interview*

1. In the first part of the interview, the counselor used several different nonverbal gestures (smiling, head-nodding, hand movement, etc.) to help put the client at ease.

Yes   No   N/A

2. In starting the interview the counselor remained silent or invited the client to talk about whatever he wanted, thus leaving the selection of initial topic up to the client.

Yes   No   N/A

3. After the first 5 minutes of the interview, the counselor refrained from encouraging social conversation.

Yes   No   N/A

4. After the first topic of discussion was exhausted, the counselor remained silent until the client identified a new topic.

Yes   No   N/A

5. The counselor provided structure (information about nature, purposes of counseling, time limits, etc.) when the client indicated uncertainty about the interview.

Yes   No   N/A

6. In beginning the *initial* interview, the counselor used at least one of the following structuring procedures:

   a. provided information about taping and/or observation
   b. commented on confidentiality
   c. made remarks about the counselor's role and purpose of the interview
   d. discussed with the client his expectations about counseling.

Yes   No   N/A

PART III: *Termination of the Interview*

1. The counselor informed the client before terminating that the interview was almost over.

   Yes   No   N/A

2. The counselor refrained from introducing new material (a different topic) at the termination phase of the interview.

   Yes   No   N/A

3. The counselor discouraged the client from pursuing new topics within the last five minutes of the interview by avoiding asking for further information about it.

   Yes   No   N/A

4. Only one attempt to terminate the interview was required before the termination was actually completed.

   Yes   No   N/A

5. The counselor initiated the termination of the interview through use of some closing strategy such as acknowledgment of time limits and/or summarization (by self or client).

   Yes   No   N/A

6. At the end of the interview, the counselor offered the client an opportunity to return for another interview.

   Yes   No   N/A

PART IV: *Goal Setting*

1. The counselor asked the client to identify some of the conditions surrounding the occurrence of the client's problem (*When* do you feel _____?).

   Yes   No   N/A

2. The counselor asked the client to identify some of the consequences resulting from the client's behavior (What happens when you _____?).

   Yes   No   N/A

3. The counselor asked the client to state how he would like to change his behavior (How would you like for things to be different?).

   Yes   No   N/A

4. The counselor and client decided *together* upon counseling goals.

   Yes   No   N/A

5. The goals set in the interview were specific and observable.

   Yes   No   N/A

6. The counselor asked the client to verbally state his commitment to work for goal achievement.

   Yes   No   N/A

7. If the client appeared resistant or unconcerned about achieving change, the counselor discussed this with him.

    Yes   No   N/A

8. The counselor asked the client to specify at least one action step he might take toward his goal.

    Yes   No   N/A

9. The counselor suggested alternatives available to the client.

    Yes   No   N/A

10. The counselor helped the client to develop action steps for goal attainment.

    Yes   No   N/A

11. Action steps designated by counselor and client were specific and realistic in scope.

    Yes   No   N/A

12. The counselor provided an opportunity within the interview for the client to practice or rehearse the action step.

    Yes   No   N/A

13. The counselor provided feedback to the client concerning the execution of the action step.

    Yes   No   N/A

14. The counselor encouraged the client to observe and evaluate the progress and outcomes of action steps taken outside the interview.

    Yes   No   N/A

PART V: *Counselor Discrimination*

1. The counselor's responses were usually directed toward the most important component of *each* of the client's communications.

    Yes   No   N/A

2. The counselor followed client topic changes by responding to the primary cognitive or affective idea reflecting a common theme in each communication.

    Yes   No   N/A

3. The counselor usually identified and responded to the feelings of the client.

    Yes   No   N/A

4. The counselor usually identified and responded to the behaviors of the client.

    Yes   No   N/A

5. The counselor verbally acknowledged several (at least two) client nonverbal affect cues.

    Yes   No   N/A

6. The counselor encouraged the client to talk about his feelings.

   Yes   No   N/A

7. The counselor encouraged the client to identify and evaluate his actions.

   Yes   No   N/A

8. The counselor discouraged the client from making and accepting excuses (rationalization) for his behavior.

   Yes   No   N/A

9. The counselor asked questions which the client couldn't answer in a yes or no fashion (typically beginning with words such as how, what, when, where, who, etc.).

   Yes   No   N/A

10. Several times (at least two) the counselor confronted the client with a discrepancy present in the client's communication and/or behavior.

   Yes   No   N/A

11. Several times (at least two) the counselor used responses that supported or reinforced something the client said or did.

   Yes   No   N/A

12. The counselor used several (at least two) responses that suggested a course of action the client had the potential for completing in the future.

   Yes   No   N/A

13. Sometimes the counselor restated or clarified the client's previous communication.

   Yes   No   N/A

14. The counselor used several (at least two) responses that summarized ambivalent and conflicting feelings of the client.

   Yes   No   N/A

15. The counselor encouraged discussion of negative feelings (anger, fear) expressed by the client.

   Yes   No   N/A

16. Several times (at least two) the counselor suggested how the client might feel about a particular topic.

   Yes   No   N/A

PART VI: *The Process of Relating*

1. The counselor made statements that reflected the client's feelings.

   Yes   No   N/A

2. The counselor responded to the core of a long and ambivalent client statement.

   Yes   No   N/A

3. The counselor verbally stated his desire and/or intent to understand.

    Yes   No   N/A

4. The counselor made verbal statements that the client reaffirmed without qualifying or changing the counselor's previous response.

    Yes   No   N/A

5. The counselor made attempts to verbally communicate his understanding of the client that elicited an affirmative client response. ("Yes, that's exactly right," and so forth).

    Yes   No   N/A

6. The counselor reflected the client's feelings at the same or a greater level of intensity than originally expressed by the client.

    Yes   No   N/A

7. In communicating understanding of the client's feelings, the counselor verbalized the anticipation present in the client's communication, i.e., what the client would like to do or how the client would like to be.

    Yes   No   N/A

8. The counselor frowned when he didn't understand what the client was saying.

    Yes   No   N/A

9. The counselor verbalized his confusion or misunderstanding to the client.

    Yes   No   N/A

10. The counselor nodded when agreeing with or encouraging the client.

    Yes   No   N/A

11. When the counselor's nonverbal behavior suggested that he was uncertain or disagreeing, the counselor verbally acknowledged this to the client.

    Yes   No   N/A

12. The counselor answered directly when the client asked about his opinion or reaction.

    Yes   No   N/A

13. The counselor encouraged discussion of statements made by the client that challenged the counselor's knowledge and beliefs.

    Yes   No   N/A

14. Several times (at least twice) the counselor shared his own feelings with the client.

    Yes   No   N/A

15. At least one time during the interview the counselor provided specific feedback to the client.

    Yes   No   N/A

16. The counselor encouraged the client to identify and discuss his feelings concerning the counselor and the interview.

    Yes   No   N/A

17. The counselor voluntarily shared his feelings about the client and the counseling relationship.

    Yes   No   N/A

18. The counselor expressed his reactions about the client's strengths and/or potential.

    Yes   No   N/A

19. The counselor made responses that reflected his liking and appreciation of the client.

    Yes   No   N/A

It is now time for us to terminate our relationship with you. The intensity that has gone into our efforts to record some meaningful suggestions makes it difficult now for us to let go. We have had this feeling before, when we entered the termination phase of a counseling relationship. You will experience the feeling also, as you move into the counseling profession. It is a sweet-and-sour consequence to achieve your goal only to find that achievement meant the end of a pleasant task.

We would like to make one final pitch as we conclude. If you are to make a difference in your helping relationships with others, it means helping others to change their lives in such a way as to make the consequence of their living more satisfying. You and your clients are more likely to succeed if you set down goals that are relevant to the client's concerns, develop strategies that are determined by those goals, and finally, assess your progress continually as you work together toward those goals. We wish you well.

Index